ESSENTIAL
PSYCHOLOGY

General Editor
Peter Herriot

G000067850

COGNITIVE
DEVELOPMENT

Johanna Turner's book . . . follows the cognitive development of children in perception, thinking and language
development in a way which not only gives examination-
passing material but also adopts a more or less consistent
viewpoint throughout and gives some genuine enlighten-
ment on the subject matter.
      John Rowan, Times Educational Supplement

*   *   *   *   *

. . . the main value of the series is that it enlarges the
variety of good quality, easily accessible books about
psychology; and thereby increases the chances of catching
a student's serious interest in 'the proper study of man-
kind'.   **Ian Hunter, Times Literary Supplement**

These short introductions will be found invaluable both by
students of psychology and also by students reading other
subjects for whom some knowledge of psychology is
essential.   **Anthony Storr, Sunday Times**

ESSENTIAL

PSYCHOLOGY

COGNITIVE DEVELOPMENT

Johanna Turner

Methuen

To my husband Roy and our children,

Alison, Roger, Simon,

Gavin and Joanna

First published 1975 by Methuen & Co Ltd
11 New Fetter Lane, London EC4P 4EE
Reprinted 1977
© Johanna Turner
Printed in Great Britain by
Richard Clay (The Chaucer Press), Ltd
Bungay, Suffolk

ISBN (hardback) 0 416 81830 7
ISBN (paperback) 0 416 81840 4

We are grateful to Grant McIntyre
of Open Books Publishing Ltd for assistance
in the preparation of this series

Contents

Acknowledgements

I would like to thank my colleagues at the University of Sussex for their comments, criticisms, and support. I am particularly indebted to Professor Hans Furth and Mr Roger Goodwin for reading portions of the manuscript and making constructive suggestions. I am most grateful to the secretarial staff of the School of Cultural and Community Studies for their goodnatured co-operation.

The publishers and I would also like to thank the following for permission to reproduce some of the figures and tables in the text (for full bibliographic details please see References and name index):

The American Psychological Association and the authors for figs 2.1 and 2.2 reprinted from H. and T. S. Kendler (1962); George Allen and Unwin and the author for fig. 2.3 reprinted from J. S. Bruner (1973); The Society for Research in Child Development and the authors for fig 3.1 and table 3.A reprinted from J. F. Wohlwill (1962), and figs 3.4, 3.5 and 3.7 reprinted from E. J. Gibson (1963); W. H. Freeman and Co. for fig. 3.6 reprinted from Robert L. Fantz (1961), and fig. 3.8 reprinted from T. G. R. Bower (1974); John Wiley and Sons for fig 4.1 reprinted from J. S. Bruner, J. S. Goodnow and G. A. Austin (1956), and fig. 4.2 reprinted from J. S. Bruner, R. R. Olver and P. M. Greenfield (1966); Holt, Rinehart and Winston and the author for table 4.A reprinted from D. M. G. Hyde (1970) and for tables 6.A and 6.B from C. A. Ferguson and D. I. Slobin (eds) (1973); Academic Press and Susan M. Ervin-Tripp for table 5.B reprinted from Timothy E. Moore (ed.) (1973); International Arts and Sciences

Press for fig. 6.1 reprinted from C. A. Ferguson and D. I. Slobin (eds) (1973); Routledge and Kegan Paul and the authors for table 7.A reprinted from W. S. Brandis and D. Henderson (1970).

Editor's Introduction

One thing of which most of us are convinced is that children think in vastly different ways from ourselves. We have to try not only to describe these differences but also to account for the progression from child to adult thinking. To use Johanna Turner's words, we have to account for 'the development of the process or processes by means of which an individual is able to acquire knowledge'. Given such a complex problem it is hardly surprising that psychologists using one particular set of concepts only as their stock-in-trade have been found wanting. The author pulls together the best of each approach. She stresses that we have to discover the ways in which people resemble each other in the stages of development through which they pass; and yet we have to account for the fact that each individual is different. She concentrates on the nature of the relation between the individual and his environment as the source of both similarities and differences. She discusses finally how language develops; here is a splendid example of a common code being acquired by individuals whose different experiences result in different language uses; but in one sense, they all share the same language.

This book belongs to Unit C of *Essential Psychology*. What unifies the titles in this unit is the concept of development. It is a very rich concept, embodying as it does the notions of process and change, and the interaction of a human being with his environment throughout his life. The individual has to maintain some sort of equilibrium between the demands of the environment and his own way of constructing reality. He has to adapt to the realities of the particular culture he lives in; but at the same time, he may be able to change his environment to a certain extent. In this way, equilibrium may be maintained without compromising his own conceptual system. The concept of development is thus ideal for dealing with growing up and changing in society. We can use the phrase 'personal development' to talk both about children and about adults; this may help us to see both as people. The reader will find other conceptual frameworks in other units. They are not so much mutually contradictory as efforts to do justice to the complexities of psychology's subject matter. Coming to terms with a variety of explanatory frameworks decreases our confidence in psychology as a mature science; but perhaps it is better to be honest about what we don't know.

Essential Psychology as a whole is designed to reflect the changing structure and function of psychology. The authors are both academics and professionals, and their aim has been to introduce the most important concepts in their areas to beginning students. They have tried to do so clearly but have not attempted to conceal the fact that concepts that now appear central to their work may soon be peripheral. In other words, they have presented psychology as a developing set of views of man, not as a body of received truth. Readers are not intended to study the whole series in order to 'master the basics'. Rather, since different people may wish to use different theoretical frameworks for their own purposes, the series has been designed so that each title stands on its own. But it is possible that if the reader has read no psychology before, he will enjoy individual books more if he has read the introductions (A1, B1, etc.) to the units to which they belong. Readers of the units concerned with applications of psychology (E, F) may benefit from reading all the introductions.

A word about references in the text to the work of other writers – e.g. (Smith, 1974). These occur where the author feels he must acknowledge an important concept or some crucial evidence by name. The book or article referred to will be listed in the References (which double as Name Index) at the back of the book. The reader is invited to consult these sources if he wishes to explore topics further. A list of general further reading is also to be found at the back of this book.

We hope you enjoy psychology.

Peter Herriot

Introduction

'When I was a child, I spoke like a child, I thought like a child, I reasoned like a child; when I became a man I gave up childish ways.' (1 Corinthians 13.8.)

But what exactly is meant by being 'a child'? Different ages have stressed different aspects of childhood and the way children are treated is largely a function of how they are defined. This book is concerned with the way a child perceives, thinks, and speaks; that is with the fundamental processes by means of which he acquires knowledge of his material and social environment and hence enters into his human inheritance. The nature of these processes has caused considerable controversy which has resulted in the various theories of cognitive development. Firstly, the child can be viewed as an organism which grows, almost like a plant, with the implication that it contains within it the seeds of adulthood and the task of the parent or teacher is to provide the environment in which these seeds can flourish. Alternatively the child can be thought to bring nothing with him beyond a set of reflexes so that what he becomes is a reflection of what has happened to him. The main difference between these two views is that the first sees the child as an active partner in his own learning whereas the second implies passivity. A third view is the 'cognitive developmental' which is essentially interactionist in that the child is here thought to be affected by the environment and yet to be able to determine, to an extent, those aspects of the environment to which he will respond. It is this third view which is most fully represented in this book.

Cognitive development is the development of a set of fundamental processes not the acquisition of any specific piece of knowledge or information. When the human baby is born it is thought to have not only reflex responses but also the propensity for attending to some aspects of the environment in preference to others. That is the baby is more sensitive to certain stimuli. Gradually the infant differentiates himself from others and begins to appreciate the nature of the world in which he finds himself, for example he learns that objects have an existence which is independent of his actions towards them. In the first two years what he perceives determines what he thinks but gradually he becomes able to think about actions, objects, and events which are not present and the perceptually dominated world of the infant becomes the conceptual world of the child and the adult.

This book begins by considering various theories of cognitive development which differ mainly in the extent to which they stress the relative importance of the child or the environment. Jean Piaget's work is treated in some detail since he has had considerable influence on both psychologists and educationists. Perceptual and conceptual development are then described with particular emphasis on infancy and the early years. The last three chapters are devoted to the development of language with certain aspects being covered in greater detail. Although several theoretical positions are included the 'cognitive developmental' is given more weight and it should be appreciated that this is merely *one* approach to a complex area.

The experiments described have been selected because they are (a) classical experiments which have stimulated subsequent studies, (b) studies which represent recent thinking on a particular subject, or (c) experiments which, either because of the neatness of their methods or the implications of their results, are of particular interest in their own right. However all selections are necessarily inadequate and to gain a more complete picture it is essential for this selection to be complemented by further reading.

The aim of this book is to introduce certain basic ideas of cognitive development to those who have no previous knowledge of the subject and it is to be hoped that even a slight acquaintance with this, the most fundamental of all aspects of human behaviour, will stimulate an interest in cognitive processes in general and engender a respect for the unique mind of every child.

I
Theoretical approaches to cognitive development: I
Jean Piaget

Theoretical background

Jean Piaget is the major exponent of the 'cognitive developmental' approach. He is concerned with the qualitative changes which take place in a person's mental make-up between birth and maturity. He maintains, firstly, that the human organism, like all other biological entities, has a characteristic internal organization; secondly, that this internal organization is responsible for the organism's unique mode of functioning, which is 'invariant', that is, it is always present and does not change over time, so that both the infant and the adult share the same *mode* of cognitive functioning; thirdly, he maintains that as a result of contact between the organism and the environment, by means of the invariant functions, the organism adapts its cognitive structures. These three postulates: internal organization, invariant functions, and interaction between organism and environment are fundamental to Piaget's position. Stated baldly they may sound abstract and abstruse but an analogy may make them clearer: every person has a digestive system which is organized in a special way so that when a person swallows food the digestive system acts upon this food which is then broken down and distributed throughout the body. However, the nature of the food also affects the body: fattening foods will cause the body to increase in weight, poison will kill it. With respect to cognition, the organism has a cognitive system which is an organized system as the digestive system is an organized system; the environment is analagous to the food taken in, which both affects the organism and is affected by it; the final cognitive structures are like the final state of the body, that is, they are a result both of the invariant functions (digestive processes) and environmental influences (the food).

Thus cognitive development, according to Piaget, is neither the result of the maturation of the organism, nor of the influence of the environment alone, but of the interaction of the two. The very word 'interaction' draws attention to the fact that the organism has an active relationship with the environment. Its actions, or better, the adaptations of its actions towards the objects in the environment are what is meant by 'cognition', which is therefore a dynamic interactic process.

For Piaget (1953:3) 'Intelligence is an adaptation'. Biologically the organism adapts itself to the environment by action and 'intelligence extends this creation by constructing mental structures which can be applied to those of the environment'. In summary he is concerned with the 'relation of thought to things'. (1953:4) There are, he says, the 'invariant functions', which we have mentioned, and the 'variant cognitive structures' – i.e. the structures change as the organism develops. It is the 'variant cognitive structures' which mark the differences between child and adult thought. But what exactly does he mean by the 'invariant functions' and the 'variant cognitive structures'?

Let us look at the invariant function called 'adaptation'. This can be subdivided into 'assimilation' and 'accommodation'. 'Assimilation' means that the organism takes in that which is external in accordance with its internal organization, just as the digestive system can assimilate animal fats but not large pieces of metal. As Piaget says, 'Intelligence is assimilation to the extent that it incorporates all the given data of experience within its framework' (1953:6). At the same time the organism 'accommodates' itself to what it has 'assimilated', as the food is used, stored, or excreted. The organism changes by assimilating the external and accommodating itself to this assimilation. Thus, 'intellectual adaptation, like every other kind, consists of putting an assimilatory mechanism and a complementary accommodation into progressive equilibrium'. (1953:7)

We have now introduced a new term 'equilibrium' which has great significance for Piaget but which cannot be understood without first explaining what he means by the 'variant cognitive structures'. Piaget is most concerned with the development of knowledge and, for him, the source of knowledge is action. Initially, the organism acts when it comes into contact with the environment. These initial actions are all overt and swiftly become co-ordinated into sets – for example the set of actions related to sucking. These sets of co-ordinated actions form what he calls 'schemes', frequently translated as 'schemas'. The various schemes which the organism has developed at any particular time form a 'structure'. Thus there is a progression from reflex scheme, to sensori-motor scheme, to structure. Bärbel Inhelder, who has worked with Piaget for many years, says that 'Some commentators refer to Piaget as "an activist", reflecting Goethe's assertion that "In the beginning was the deed" '. (1962: 21) She herself says:

the development of knowledge seems to be the result of a process of elaboration that is based essentially on the activity of the child . . . it is thus in acting on the external world that according to Piaget, the child elaborates a more and more adequate knowledge of reality. It is precisely the successive forms of his activity in the course of his development that determine his modes of knowledge. (1962:20)

As the organism develops, its cognitive structures change from the 'instinctual' through the 'sensori-motor' to the 'operational' structure of adult thought and Piaget maintains that these three forms of cognitive structure represent three different levels of knowing. Thus knowledge is not a thing which the organism takes in but a process by means of which it makes sense of its environment – it is the organism's active adaptation either by overt or internalized actions. Thus the schemes of overt actions of the first stage become the schemes of internalized actions or 'operations' of the later stage. If the source of knowledge is action it becomes apparent that each level of knowing is character-ized by different forms of action towards the objects in the environment.

We can now return to the term 'equilibrium' and the process of 'equilibration'. Briefly, the organism has, at any point in time, a set of schemes capable of dealing with the environment. Then an environmental situation demonstrates that the present schemes have developed to a point where they are inadequate to cope with the newly discovered situation and the organism is thrown into disequilibrium, so it adapts its scheme to the new situation and equilibrium is restored. This process of restoring equilibrium is known as 'equilibration'. Equilibrium is not a static state, rather it represents an 'active system of compensations' (Inhelder, 1962:28). The organism is therefore self-regulative as well as active.

Thus Piaget hypothesizes how cognition develops and he further claims that this developmental process is marked by a series of stages, the order of which is invariant although the age of onset and termination may vary. He is not saying that a person functions exclusively at one stage – indeed a child or adult may operate at one level for one concept and at a higher or lower level for another. But, generally speaking, each stage represents a different way of dealing with a particular aspect of the environment and hence one would expect that most of a child's thinking would be characteristic of the stage he has reached. Piaget distinguishes four main stages: sensori-motor (0–2 years), pre-operational (2–7 years), concrete operational (7–11 years), and formal operational (11–adulthood).

The sensori-motor stage (0–2)

During these first two years the infant is making enormous cognitive strides. Why does he learn? His motivation is, as we have seen, the occurrence of an event which is experienced as causing some disturbance to the existing schemes. This is assimilated and the infant accommodates its structures, thereby developing new structures, and equilibrium is restored. How does he learn? At the sensori-motor level there is no distinction between perceiving a thing and acting in response to it: at this stage thought is, literally, action and to understand a major distinction between this early stage and the later stages it is necessary to introduce two new terms, namely the 'figurative' and 'operative' aspects of knowing. 'Figurative' knowing merely takes account of the immediate aspects of a situation or object in so far as its aspects are observable to the person, whereas 'operative' knowing goes beyond the immediate and transforms or interprets that which is perceived in accordance with the cognitive structures which have been developed. As at the sensori-motor stage perception is not separated from action then the figurative and the operative aspects are undifferentiated, but subsequent development enables the child to separate perception and action and hence to separate figurative and operative knowing. The infant thus develops by initially acting towards the immediately perceived environment and subsequently by beginning to internalize these actions so that he can for example think about his coming meal although no meal is present.

Piaget's method was closely to observe children and most of his empirical data for the sensori-motor period was obtained by the observation of his three children. At birth the infant exhibits a limited range of un-coordinated reflexes which are a necessary condition for any subsequent development. The first four months show the start of adaptation. Initially the infant's adaptive action may be a chance matter but it will then be repeated until gradually a new scheme develops or two schemes are co-ordinated. Piaget calls this process a 'circular reaction'. In these early months primary circular reactions enable the infant to move from the reflex sucking scheme to the more differentiated sensori–motor scheme of sucking his fingers or from seeing an object and touching an object separately to grasping an object he can see.

Between four and eight months 'secondary circular reactions' develop by means of which the infant is able to act upon his environment in an instrumental way: if his activities cause a change in the environment, e.g. a noise or an interesting sight, he can by his own action cause the interesting sound or sight either to recur or to be maintained in existence. These secondary circular reactions then become co-ordinated to form more complex schemes which show that intentionality is beginning to develop: the infant, for example, begins to search for hidden objects and becomes interested in new things just because they are new. A behaviour pattern typical of this age is portrayed in Piaget's description of his daughter Jacqueline's behaviour when she was eight months (figures in brackets refer to the age of the child, thus 0·8 (8) means eight months and eight days):

Observation 127 – If Jacqueline at 0·8 (8) has shown herself capable of removing a hand which forms an obstacle to her desires, she has not delayed in making herself capable of the inverse behaviour pattern; using the other person's hand as an intermediate in order to produce a coveted result. Thus at 0·8 (13) Jacqueline looks at her mother who is swinging a flounce of material with her hand. When this spectacle is over Jacqueline, instead of imitating the movement which she will do shortly thereafter, begins to search for her mother's hand, places it in front of the flounce, and pushes it to make it resume its activity. (1953:223)

During the second year the child moves from this 'logic of action' to representing events which are not perceptually present. He moves from overt physical actions to covert internalized actions which we can call 'pre-operations', and becomes capable of thinking about doing X rather than actually performing the physical manipulations. This new skill is evinced in the infant's changed orientation towards objects. During the second year the child begins to realize that objects exist independently of his actions towards them; this is the embryonic stage of abstract thought. The sensori-motor stage is said to have ended when the infant is able to represent what he knows symbolically, so that what he knows is no longer tied to what he does.

This is a particularly important development and needs to be clearly understood. To be able to think symbolically means that

17

the child must be able to represent an event in his mind and internally reflect upon it. His whole world is extended in that he can think of something which is not present but which was or will be present. Of course, as we shall see, at this early stage his vestigial symbolic activity is weak so that his thinking lacks order and logic, he sees 'in a glass darkly' and with distortion, but his fundamental process of cognition is gaining power. As the two-year-old toddles with uneven steps his immature but ever-present cognitive capacity has already marked him out as distinct from the rest of the animal world.

The pre-operational stage (2–7)

The sensori-motor stage ends with the start of the capacity to symbolize but it is not until the child is 'operational' at about the age of seven that this capacity will be fully developed. Between the end of the sensori-motor stage and the start of the operational stage is the pre-operational stage. This stage can be thought of as a period in which children use thinking faultily, a situation which will be improved through the development of operations. This should not be seen as a negative view: pre-operational thought *is* limited and frequently mistaken from an adult perspective but it is through the resolution of these limitations that learning takes place.

What then are the characteristics of pre-operational thinking? Firstly the child, although able to distinguish between himself and objects, is not able to conceive of any other way of experiencing objects except his own way. He has just one point of view – his own and finds it difficult to adapt this to take account of the views of others. For example, when recounting something that has happened to him he cannot adapt his story to make allowances for what his listener needs to know. If he is shown a model of three mountains such that:

From his initial position in front of the model the child sees a green mountain occupying the foreground a little to his right. The summit of this mountain is topped by a little house. To his left he sees a brown mountain, higher than the green one and slightly to its rear. This mountain is distinguished not only by its colour but also by having a red cross at the summit. In the background stands the highest of the three mountains, a grey pyramid whose peak is covered in snow. (Piaget, Inhelder, 1962:211)

and is then given a doll which is placed in various positions so that it views the mountains from different angles, he is unable to point out a photograph which would correspond to the doll's

18

view, nor can he rearrange the mountain so as to reconstruct the doll's view. The child is thus 'egocentric', that is his view of the world is centred on himself – not selfishly but conceptually.

This egocentric attitude is really a particular example of a more general characteristic and that is the pre-operational child's inability to consider two aspects of the same situation at one and the same time: he will consider one, for example the perceptual, to the exclusion of all other relevant information. The well known 'beaker experiment' illustrates this. Here the child, having agreed that two short broad beakers X and Y contain the same amount of liquid, watches the experimenter pour the liquid from one of the beakers Y into a tall narrow one Z. When asked if these two beakers X and Z contain the same amount of liquid, the child will reply that Z contains more, because he is concentrating on height and neglecting width.

This experiment also illustrates a third important characteristic of pre-operational thought: its irreversibility. Having thought through a chain of reasoning A, B, C, the child cannot go back and, as it were, unwind C, B, A. There is a significant change in thinking when the child moves from repeating 'The house that Jack built' by rote (so that if he stops he is lost) to when he is able to *work out* what comes next by working backwards. It can take a child a considerable time, sometimes up till seven, to realize that if $2 + 2 = 4$, then $4 - 2 \ must = 2$. It is this element of necessity that is lacking in pre-operational thinking although often the child will give the 'right' answer through associative learning.

Thinking at this stage is fluid and easily disturbed, the child can be easily misled by observable spatial changes. If he lays out five coins and matches them with five sweets he may agree that there are the same number in each line, but if the sweets are then bunched together he will say that there are more coins. An older child may recount the sweets, showing that he too does not appreciate the element of necessity – i.e. if no sweets have been added and none taken away then the number *must* be the same.

This is indicative of the child's failure to 'conserve'. Non-conservation can be seen for example in the child's method of handling problems to do with substance, length, and area. If the child and the experimenter each have a ball of plasticine and the child agrees that each ball has the same amount in it, and if the experimenter then rolls his ball into a sausage shape or flattens it out into a pancake, the child will say that the sausage or the pancake now has more. This can be checked by using an edible material for the experiment and asking the child to choose which shape he would like to eat—once again he will choose the one that to him looks larger in some way. Similarly if two sticks of the same length are laid alongside one another so that the ends are aligned the child will say that they are the same length, but if the experimenter moves one stick an inch or so ahead of the other the child will say that the stick which has been moved has become the longer one.

Conservation of area can be tested in several ways, commonly by showing the child two pieces of green paper of equal size and telling him that these are meant to be fields. A toy cow is then put on each and the child will agree that they have the same amount of grass to eat. The experimenter then puts six model houses on each field so that on the first field they are together in a line but on the second they are in different parts of the field. The child will then say that the cow in the first field has more grass to eat, because he can see an unbroken expanse of grass. Just as the child is unable to fully understand what dimensions change and what remains constant so he is unable to work through the necessary sub-stages whereby for example vertical line AB becomes horizontal line AC (fig. 1.1).

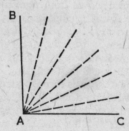

Fig. 1.1 *Comprehension of changes in orientation*

A child cannot draw the intermediate lines shown here as broken.

It is, however, not just changes of state which confuse a child of this age, he also has great difficulty when attempting to classify or seriate. Classification requires a child to be able to conceive of object X belonging to more than one class at one and the same time and as forming a subordinate class of a larger superordinate class. For example if the child is shown some red circles, red squares, blue circles and blue squares, he has difficulty in separating out the four overlapping classes of circles (both red and blue), squares (both red and blue), red objects (both square and circular) and blue objects (both square and circular). Similarly he can divide flowers into red flowers and blue flowers but if he is shown a bunch consisting of five red and four blue flowers and asked 'are there more red flowers or more flowers?' he will reply 'more red flowers' since he does not realize that the subordinate classes 'red flowers' and 'blue flowers' are included in the superordinate class of 'flowers'.

Seriation requires a different type of understanding. To test this the child is asked to construct a 'staircase' with rods of graduated lengths, or he is asked to insert one or more rods into a semi-complete staircase. Initially the child can only seriate one of two rods, by age five or six the staircase is completed but new rods are fitted in by trial and error. It is not till seven or eight that the series is completed by starting with the longest or shortest rod, looking for the next and then the next until all are in place. This requires the child not to be confused by the fact that rod C is both longer than rod B and shorter than rod D.

Finally, since the pre-operational child's thinking is still closely tied to action it is unduly realistic in that, for example, the name of an object is thought of as a property of that object. This extreme concreteness is illustrated by a story the Russian psychologist Vygotsky tells when he is making a similar point:

> In one experiment the children were told that in a game a dog would be called 'cow'. Here is a typical example of questions and answers:
> 'Does a cow have horns?'
> 'Yes.'
> 'But don't you remember that a cow is really a dog. Come now does a dog have horns?'
> 'Sure, if it is a cow, if it's called cow, it has horns. That kind of dog has got to have little horns'. (1962: 129)

Pre-operational thinking is thus 'intuitive': things are as they seem to be rather than as they must be. The development of operations enables the child to go beyond his own experience and beyond appearances.

Operational stages (concrete and formal)

The development of operations lasts from seven to sixteen and has two sub-stages: 'concrete operations' from seven to eleven or twelve and 'formal operations' from twelve onwards. During the concrete period the child's thought becomes less egocentric, less fluid, and more reversible so that he is now able to take several aspects of a situation into account. He begins to develop coherent cognitive schemes which are, initially, sequences of actions. The most important aspect of operational thinking is that it is reversible and the child now, because he is more systematic, is not so easily misled as he was in the pre-operational period.

In the period of concrete operations Piaget for the first time is able to describe cognitive functioning in terms of logico-mathematical structure:

> I analysed in children four to seven or eight years of age the relationship of part and whole. . . . These studies led me to understand why logical and mathematical operations cannot be formed independently; the child can grasp a certain operation only if he is capable, at the same time, of correlating operations by modifying them in different well determined ways, for instance by inverting them. These operations presuppose, as does any primary intelligent conduct, the possibility of making detours (which corresponds to what logicians call 'associativity') and returns '(reversibility') . . . I sought for the most elementary operative structures of the whole and I finally found them in the mental processes underlying the formation of the idea of preservation or constancy . . . such structures represent the most primitive parts of a part-whole organization: I have called them 'groupings'. (Boring, 1952:252)

Different groupings are thought to underlie concrete thinking and Piaget distinguishes logical from infra-logical groupings, the former involve logical classes, the latter the relationships between parts and wholes – such as 'greater than' or 'less than'.

Grouping 1 has been thoroughly studied by Piaget and Inhelder in connection with classification. It describes the inclusion of one class within another, which is in its turn part of another, until the largest class is reached which includes all the members of the set. For example:

$$A + A_1 = B \text{ i.e. Sussex men} + \text{men from all the other counties}$$
$$= \text{Englishmen}$$
$$B + B_1 = C \text{ i.e. Englishman} + \text{Irish, Scots and Welshmen}$$
$$= \text{British men}$$
$$C + C_1 = D \text{ i.e. British men} + \text{all the men in the other European states}$$
$$= \text{European men}$$
$$D + D_1 = E \text{ i.e. European men} + \text{men from the four other continents}$$
$$= \text{all men}$$

Piaget and Inhelder describe empirical studies designed to test a child's understanding of this additive classification system. The child is given objects which vary along the dimensions of shape, colour and material so that the child when asked to 'put together the things that are alike' is able to use any of these attributes as the basis for his classification. The youngest children show fluid chaining collections, a red circle followed by a red square, followed by a blue square etc. or they make 'graphic' collections which look like something with which the child is familiar – a train or a boat for instance. They then make small collections the basis of which resides in the child's own experience and not in the properties of the object, for instance a table may be put with a chair but a bed would not be included in the set because the child is not thinking of 'furniture'. Finally the child is able to classify correctly, but even up to age seven or eight, if he has, for example, chosen shape as the basis of his classification, he will have difficulty reclassifying using colour as the criterion.

Piaget considers that an understanding of the 'all' – 'some' relationship is crucial for classifying and he did one particularly illuminating experiment. In this the child was given blue squares, red squares, and blue circles. He was then asked, 'Are all the circles blue?' or told that 'Tony said all the circles were blue. Now, what do you think? Was Tony right?' A typical reply from a child before the concrete stage would be 'No, Tony was wrong, because there are also blue squares' as if he were answering 'Are all the blue ones circular?' As Inhelder remarks:

> The quantitative aspect of the logical concept of class inclusion, in which if all A is B then B includes A (B > A), depends upon the prior formation – full of snares and pitfalls – of a hierarchical system of classes. (1962: 32)

During the concrete stage the child's thinking encompasses the nine groupings described by Piaget but he is still limited, in particular he cannot deal with abstract combinatorial systems nor understand the notion of the experimental manipulation of one variable at a time and then the combination of variables. For example if the experimenter says 'Whenever my dog eats liver and bacon, he is ill. What do you think is the cause of it?', the child is unable to work out that it might be the liver or it might be the bacon or it might be the combination of liver with bacon.

The change from concrete to formal operations marks a fundamental change in the child's attitude towards problem-solving. Concrete operations deal directly with objects but formal operations extend concrete systems to include ideas of combination and possibility due to the child's becoming aware of the interdependence of variables such as weight, speed, and time which had previously been considered in isolation. The child, having formed the discrete, separate, distinct concrete structures, begins, once he has realized their interdependence, to unite them in various ways, and it is the integrated structure of formal thought which makes it unique:

> thinking becomes formal as soon as it undertakes the co-ordination of concrete groupings into a single system . . . because it deals with possible combinations and no longer with objects directly. (Piaget, 1958:292–3)

The child is now able to distinguish and order all the possible combinations of units of data so that if he has four variables he can generate the sixteen possible combinations of them. The formally operational person can also consider possible worlds as well as the actual world before him and hence think hypothetically.

With the emergence of formal thought the long process of cognitive development is complete but we should not assume that all adults achieve formal thought nor that the whole of an adult's thinking is always formal.

Further theoretical considerations

Having considered Piaget's theory in general and briefly summarized the characteristics of the developmental stages, we must now turn to his definitions of 'intelligence' and 'thinking', the distinction between 'learning' and 'development', and, finally, Piaget's views of the relationship between language and thought.

For Piaget 'intelligence' is the sum total of all the cognitive structures any person has developed at any particular moment, hence he can speak of 'sensori-motor' or 'pre-operational' intelligence. It is, however, 'operational' intelligence which approximates most closely to what we normally understand by this term. He has also considered the controversial question of the hereditability of intelligence and argues that there are two groups of hereditary factors:

> The hereditary factors of the first group are structural and are connected with the constitution of our nervous system and sensory organs. Thus we perceive certain physical radiations, but not all of them, and matter only of a certain size etc. Now these known structural factors influence the building up of our most fundamental concepts . . . These characteristics of the first type, while supplying the intelligence with useful structures, are thus essentially limited. . . . In contrast, the deductive and organizing activity of the mind is unlimited and leads, in the realm of space, precisely to generalizations which surpass intuition. To the extent that this activity of the mind is hereditary it is so in quite a different sense from the former group. (1953:1–2)

In February 1969 the California Test Bureau sponsored a conference to consider the implications of Piaget's theory for the development of ordinal scales of cognitive development. David Elkins neatly summarizes the difference between the approach of those who are concerned with I.Q. in the sense of what I.Q. tests measure and Piaget's views of the nature of intelligence by saying that mental growth for the former is a statistical concept reflecting rate of growth whereas the latter sees mental growth as reflecting the formation of new mental structures. He draws attention to the different purpose of the studies:

> Mental tests were practical tools whose use could be justified on the basis of the fact that they worked and did the job they were supposed to do. Piaget's tasks, in contrast, were designed to test his hypotheses regarding how the child obtains certain concepts. (Green, 1971:26)

This leads him to conclude that at present Piagetian tasks are not suitable for inclusion in intelligence testing in preference to tests already in use. However, the British Intelligence Scale is including items based on Piagetian thinking as it is hoped that such items will help to contribute to a more complete assessment of the child's ability. Donald Ross picks this point up when, in summarizing the conference he points out that a Piaget task could give 'a real indication of what. . . . he could do intellectually . . . it would not be necessary to say whether the person was better or worse than anyone else! (Green, 1971:216)

'Thinking' for Piaget is nothing else but 'operational' intelligence, hence sensori-motor and pre-operational behaviour can be contrasted with mature 'thinking' behaviour since at the early stage thinking is action. This is an unusual usage of the word 'thinking'. His use of 'learning' is similarly limited in that he uses it when referring to the acquisition of a specific piece of information. For example, through the development of intelligence the child becomes *able* to classify the various species of animals but he needs to *learn* the correct place in the classificatory hierarchy of any particular species. Before he is operational he will not be able to include whales and humans in the superordinate category of mammals, but unless he has learnt what a mammal is and that a whale is one, even being at the formal stage will not enable his intelligence to tell him this – he has to learn it. Alternatively, a pre-operational child may 'learn' in a particular case that if John is taller than Bill and Bill is taller than Peter, then John is taller than Peter, but until he has developed the appropriate cognitive structure he will not realize that this will always be the case irrespective of the particular people involved. Thus intelligence is a necessary but not sufficient condition for learning but learning a particular content is neither necessary nor sufficient for the development of intelligence, which, as we have seen, develops through the process of equilibration.

What then is the relationship between language and thought? By now it should be fairly clear that if thinking is the result of operational intelligence which does not begin to develop until the age of seven, then the appearance of language precedes the appearance of thought by several years. This has, according to Piaget, two consequences: firstly, the ability of language to facilitate thinking, contrary to what is often assumed, is greatest after the appearance of operational thinking, and especially during the stage of formal operations. Secondly, in the earlier stages, language, since it is a symbolic system, is less important as an aid to intelligence than is often thought. It is true that language will aid learning, as defined above, but it shows the limitation characteristic of all symbols, which is that since a symbol stands in place of the object it symbolizes, then it can only be interpreted if one *already knows* the object. Therefore symbols do not add anything new to an individual's knowledge, they merely enable him to formulate what he already knows in a different way. To be able to use a symbolic form of expression, for example saying 'I want my doll' instead of being limited to the action of pointing, is the *result* of the development of the schemes which end the sensori-motor stage, not the cause of their development. However, since language, by its very nature, enables a person to transcend the here and now, it is particularly appropriate as the vehicle for formal thought which, again by its very nature, is concerned with possible rather than actual worlds and with the hypothetical rather than the verified.

Over the past half century Piaget has made a major contribution to our understanding of cognitive development but it makes a travesty of his thinking to concentrate on the characteristics of the stages and neglect his theory of the development of knowledge which is what is illustrated by these characteristic stage behaviours. Piaget lays before us a theory based on biological functioning which stresses that cognitive development is the result of the organism's active adaptation to the environment through accommodation and assimilation. As a result of this the variant cognitive structures develop, which are themselves co-ordinated schemes, and which, in turn, combine to form intelligence. Intelligence, at the operational level, is thinking, and both intelligence and thinking have to be distinguished from learning.

This theory then has particular and radical implications for the role of language in thinking. Piaget is not easy to understand, nor may one always agree with his interpretations of the empirical data, but no scientific perspective can do more than approximate to truth. Piaget has made a start and it is for others to extend his insights when they, in their turn, continue thinking about thinking.

2
Theoretical approaches to cognitive development: 2

Piaget is the colossus of cognitive development, but there are a number of other important theoretical approaches. Some are less familiar, but all are worthy of consideration.

Some stimulus response theorists

Stimulus/response or S–R theorists have a different approach to that of Piaget in that their prime concern is with the overt behaviour which can be observed (see A3). They do not, in their strictest form, make inferences from overt behaviour to covert mental processes nor attempt to go beyond the actual responses exhibited in the experimental situations. Their belief is, firstly, that all behaviour is learned as the result of associating a stimulus with a response. Secondly, that a response will recur if it is positively reinforced and be inhibited if it is negatively reinforced. By this they mean that if stimulus A illicits response B in the first instance, and if response B is followed by something that is pleasant or rewarding, then when stimulus A recurs response B will recur; but if it is followed by something unpleasant the unpleasant effect will be associated with response B which will not occur again after stimulus A. (It is also possible to generalize a response so that if a subject is positively reinforced for responding to a musical note, say middle C, he will also respond to adjacent notes, or if he responds to a bell and the bell is paired with a buzzer he will learn to respond to the buzzer alone. However if the stimulus is too far removed it will not occur.) Variations in the schedules of reinforcement will vary the behaviour in that a response need not be positively reinforced every time but if it is never positively reinforced it will gradually die out i.e. be 'extinguished', whereas if it is sporadically reinforced it will tend to become firmly established since the subject will, as it were, 'live in hope'.

It is important to distinguish between the extinction of a response, that is when a response fails to occur because the association between it and the stimulus no longer exists, and when a response is inhibited by negative reinforcement. In this case the link is still there but the behaviour is not exhibited since fear or a wish to avoid the negative reinforcement inhibits it. Words like 'hope' and 'wish' are, in fact, inadmissible since they relate to mental states and it is this type of reference which these psychologists wish, by the nature of their theories, to avoid. Although this may sound simple such theories can be elaborated and provide some quite subtle insights. Perhaps their greatest strength is that the hypotheses they generate are specific enough to be experimentally tested.

The differences between the S–R approach and that of Piaget's is exemplified with Watson's S–R analysis of conservation. Suppose that in the classic conservation task, a child who had agreed that two original balls of plasticine contained the same amount, saw one ball shaped, and still said that the reshaped ball contained 'the same' amount as the non-reshaped, this response would be interpreted by the Piagetians as meaning that the child was able to conserve, whereas S–R theorists, such as B. F. Skinner, would see it as evidence that the response 'they are the same' had been positively reinforced in similar stimulus situations. In the classic conservation experiment there are three distinct parts, firstly where the balls are seen as identical; secondly, where one ball is transformed; and thirdly, where the two balls no longer appear the same. Watson expresses this: (S = situation, s = stimulus) $S.1$ $(sa = sb)$: $S.2$ $(sb \rightarrow sb_1)$: $S.3$ $(sa \neq sb_1)$, that is in situation $S.1$, stimulus a equals stimulus b; in $S.2$ stimulus b is reshaped into b_1; and in $S.3$ stimulus a no longer appears to be equal to stimulus b_1. What controls the response 'the same' in $S.3$? Watson suggests that it is $S.2$ which determines the answer in $S.3$. If nothing is added or subtracted, (condition $cS.2$), the conserver response 'the same' is given in $S.3$, whereas if something is added or subtracted, (condition $\notcS.2$) the response 'the same' is not given in $S.3$; therefore a correct response requires the subject to discriminate between $cS.2$ and $\notcS.2$. Now, Watson argues, when a child fails to reply 'the same' in $S.3$ it is taken that it is failure of conservation that is being displayed. On the contrary the child's response could indicate that he is unable to discriminate $cS.2$ from $\not{c}S.2$, that is he cannot tell whether anything has been added or subtracted. When, however, a child does conserve and says it is 'because nothing was added or taken away' the Piagetians would see this as 'a reflection of a subject's logical sophistication' whereas Watson says that he may be 'reporting his identifications of the discriminative stimulus' (1968: 452), that is having identified the situation as $cS.2$ (and as not $\not{c}S.2$) he gives the correct response to this stimulus. His reason is not inferential but merely a description of the stimulus which made the response 'the same' correct. Therefore one can distinguish between a true logical inference and a response which is the result of discriminative instrumental conditioning. Watson says that seeing the effect of varying the standard classic task may help to show which interpretation is correct.

The standard task is well known. One variant would be to add something in the transformation stage ($\not{c}S.2$), but another variant would be not to have the two stimuli in the first condition the same, that is one ball could be much smaller than the other therefore he suggests the following variations:

Standard task: $S.1$ $(sa = sb)$ $cS.2$ $(sb \rightarrow sb_1)$ $S.3$ $(sa \neq sb_1)$
Variant 1: $\quad\;\;\; S.1$ $(sa = sb)$ $\not{c}S.2$ $(sb \rightarrow sb_1)$ $S.3$ $(sa \neq sb_1)$
Variant 2: $\quad\;\;\; S.1$ $(sa \neq sb)$ $cS.2$ $(sb \rightarrow sb_1)$ $S.3$ $(sa \neq sb_1)$
Variant 3: $\quad\;\;\; S.1$ $(sa \neq sb)$ $\not{c}S.2$ $(sb \rightarrow sb_1)$ $S.3$ $(sa \neq sb_1)$
(1968:454)

In this situation the Piagetian and S–R theorists would make different predictions of what would happen to children with Variant 3, who had already responded to the Standard and Variants 1 and 2. The Piagetian theory would predict that if the children were indeed behaving logically, they would say 'I can't tell because you added something to the small one', whereas the S–R theorists would predict that if the children had learnt to say 'they are not the same' and to describe the stimulus in $S.2$ they would still say 'they are not the same' and add 'because they were not the same to begin with, the ball made into a pancake was smaller, and you added some plasticine while making the pancake'. To run an experiment of this kind would be helpful in indicating exactly what was going on in the child's mind. The S–R approach also has implications for training since, if it were correct, emphasis in training procedures would need to be on the ability to make discriminations and reward correct choices in the $S.2$ condition.

The simplest form of S–R behaviour is known as 'classical' conditioning. It stems from the work of Pavlov in which an initial simple response, for example salivation to the stimulus of meat powder, was paired with a bell. Subsequently the sound of a bell without the meat powder would cause salivation. A slightly more complex variant of S–R theories is B. F. Skinner's 'operant' conditioning. Here the experimenter waits for the subject to perform some random action. This action is then reinforced – the subject learns to perform it to obtain the reward. The simple examples of conditioning could be explained by a 'single unit' S–R theory: the stimulus and the response are directly linked. But not all learning seems explicable in these terms, despite Skinner's ingenuity.

Of more interest for cognitive development is the type of theory which abandons single unit S–R and posits an 'internal mediating response'. A classical mediation experiment is described by Miller (1948). In this experiment a rat was put into a white compartment and given electric shocks so that it learned to fear or show anxiety whenever it was placed in the white compartment. It was then put in the white compartment but one side was replaced by a hurdle over which it could jump into a black compartment. It was not shocked in the white compartment but after a few trials it learned to jump into the black compartment. Why, then, did it jump? The argument is that the white compartment caused anxiety which was assuaged by its jumping into the black and it was the reduction of this anxiety that was reinforcing. There was after all no pain to escape from. Here the reduction of anxiety is a 'mediating' response, a two-stage process has occurred.

Mediating responses, of course, cannot be directly observed, they are 'hypothetical constructs' justified by their ability to explain overt behaviour. These mediating responses are obviously particularly significant for cognitive processes, particularly with respect to words as mediators. The Kendlers, two mediation theorists, argue that the study of problem-solving requires experiments which 'isolate and magnify the basic mechanisms' (1962:2) which operate in the more complex problems of daily life and are therefore necessary conditions for their solution. They represent the behaviour in S–R terms, not, as they say, because this is how we find behaviour but because it is a convenient way of representing it. They also accept that insight is important but account for it by saying that it is the result of the fact that independent levels of behaviour occur simultaneously in independent S–R chains so that sometimes a stimulus in one chain is linked to a response in another and this 'sparking across' results in apparently insightful behaviour. They distinguish two processes:

31

one, 'the horizontal', in which behaviour is continuous; and two, 'the vertical', which refers to the above independent chains of habits occurring simultaneously.

Their most ingenious experiments have been concerned with 'reversal' and 'non-reversal' shifts (see A7). In these a subject was presented with four cups; a large black one, a large white one, a small black one, and a small white one. He first learned to respond positively to one dimension, for example size, so that large was positive and small negative. In a 'reversal shift' he has to learn to respond to the same dimension but to reverse his choice so that small becomes positive and large negative; in a 'non-reversal shift' he has to respond to the black/white dimension and ignore size so that black becomes positive and white negative

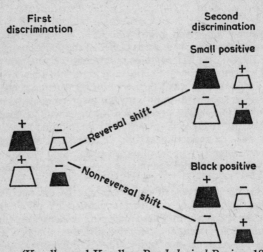

(Kendler and Kendler, *Psychological Review*, 1962)

Fig. 2.1 *Examples of a reversal and a non-reversal shift*

(fig. 2.1). Rats respond more rapidly to a non-reversal shift, college students to a reversal shift and children swop preference at about six.

A comparison of fast and slow learning kindergarten children showed that slow learners found non-reversal shifts easier, fast learners preferred reversal shifts. Why is this? The Kendlers explain it in terms of mediation theory as follows: A mediation theory hypothesizes implicit S–R events which behave as explicit S–R events. A single-unit theory will see the stimulus 'cup' leading to the response large/small in a reversal shift and large/black in a non-reversal shift. In this situation a non-reversal shift should be easier as 'black' can be added to 'large' to get a positive, whereas 'large' has to be abandoned to get 'small' positive in a reversal shift. In mediation theory the results would be reversed as the subject could use the same mediated response 'size' in a reversal shift but needs to develop a new one 'colour/brightness' in a non-reversal shift and therefore this would take

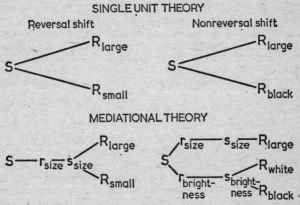

(Kendler and Kendler, *Psychological Review*, 1962)

Fig. 2.2 *A single-unit and mediational S–R analysis of a reversal and non-reversal shift*

longer (fig. 2.2.). They conclude that single-unit theory represents the behaviour of rats and young children whereas adult human behaviour cannot be adequately represented without using hypothetical constructs such as a mediating response.

Berlyne describes higher mental processes such as thinking in S–R terms but also uses a mediation theory which he refers to as 'neo-associationist'. For 'neo-associationist', internal processes can be conceptualized as 'responses' and 'stimuli' in contrast to the formulations of cognitive theorists who believe that central mediating processes such as cognitions, expectations, or images obey laws that can differ from those which govern the overt response. Berlyne defined thinking in general as any process that involves a chain of responses, and directed thinking as a form of thinking whose function is to lead to the solution of a problem. He maintained that it was possible, through symbolic mediation, to represent external stimuli and overt responses internally and hence a thinker could, as it were, go through an implicit chain of S–R situations. Thought becomes a 'symbolic response'. When a thinker represents a situation internally he may also represent internally the actions he would have to perform to change the situation, these internal representations of action are called by Berlyne 'transformational thoughts', which have a similar sound to Piaget's 'operations' but they do have all the properties of overt responses in that they have to be reinforced, and can be inhibited or extinguished:

> Transformational thoughts are conceived as derivatives of those overt responses that regularly result in particular trends of environmental change. Their possession enables the subject to represent to himself and communicate to others the stimulus situation that would result from a series of transformations, even when the transformations are not actually affected. (1965:123)

Berlyne is also concerned with what he calls 'habit family hierarchies' of stimulus and response by which he means a set of behaviour chains in which each chain begins from the same initial situation, that is the initial stimulus, and ends with the achievement of the goal that had been envisaged.

Berlyne has also produced a complementary theory of motivation, which, relying as it does on conceptual conflict, sounds very similar to Piaget's, but on closer examination turns out to be wider in conception. Every thinker has firstly to be activated; secondly, to give his thinking direction by his notion of the end to be achieved, and thirdly, to find such activity reinforcing. Of reinforcement he says 'the achievement of a symbolic sequence or pattern that the subject regards as a successful conclusion of the thinking process is clearly analogous to the attainment of a reinforcing state of affairs or a goal situation in motor learning'. (1965:242). In addition cognitive conflict is important and by cognitive conflict he (as opposed to Piaget) means an element of uncertainty caused by the juxtaposition of incompatible symbolic response patterns, that is when one pattern is associated with the inhibition of the other. He lists six types of cognitive conflicts: firstly, 'doubt' in which a person both believes and disbelieves in a proposition; secondly, 'perplexity', especially subjective uncertainty, when the person is both drawn towards and repelled by a person or a situation; thirdly, 'contradiction' which can be intense when the person is led to believe at one and the same time that X is true and X is false; fourthly, 'conceptual incongruity', when a single object possesses properties that were previously thought to be mutually exclusive (the example given by Berlyne is a mud-skipper fish, which can, apparently, walk on dry land;) fifthly, 'confusion', caused by ambiguous verbal material or by information whose implications are only partly seen by the subject; and, finally, 'irrelevance' when thoughts which seem to lead away from the solution occur through association.

To test these views Berlyne performed some studies (1954; 1962b). For example, secondary school children were given forty-eight questions on invertebrates and asked to mark the twelve for which they particularly wished to have the answers. Familiar animals caused more curiosity than non-familiar since familiar animals arouse more competitive thought. They also wanted answers to questions they found surprising or which attributed qualities to the animals which the subject did not think they possessed.

Berlyne (1962a) argues that much of Piagetian theory can be re-formulated, without loss of meaning, in S–R language. Firstly, 'equilibration' could be seen as a reinforcing process in that if the organism's schemes were inadequate it would feel discomfort, presumably a kind of 'cognitive pain', and the resolution of this discomfort, when new schemes were developed, would act as a positive reinforcer. Berlyne would find support for this view from recent work with infants which suggest that problem-solving *per se* is sufficiently reinforcing for the infant to engage in it without any other reinforcing agent. Papousek (1969) describes an experiment in which infants of two to three months could learn to turn on a light by moving their heads to the right or left. Once the infants had learnt that a turn to the left would turn on the light their response rate dropped. When the experimenter varied the schedule so that a right turn could result in the light coming on the infants would show interest and then the rate would drop again. The infants gradually learned complicated sequences like: right – right – left – left. Whenever the schedule was changed the infants showed increased activity and appeared to be trying out different series of head movements, once they had discovered the correct sequence their activity again dropped. During the trials they hardly looked at the light beyond glancing to see if it was on. Therefore it seems as if it was the problem-solving that was reinforcing and not the presence of the light.

Secondly, Berlyne suggested that Piaget's 'operations' should be viewed as 'habits subject to great S–R generalization' (1962a:128). He bases this on Hull's (1943) three types of generalizations resulting from the establishment of a bond of association between stimulus A and response B namely, (1) generalizations such that other stimuli representing stimulus A become associated with response B; (2) response generalizations such that other responses resembling response B become associated with stimulus A; and (3) stimulus response generalizations such that other stimuli resembling stimulus A become associated with other responses resembling response B (adapted from Berlyne, 1962a:128).

Thirdly, Berlyne's notion of transformational thoughts enables him to account for directed thought which is aimed at reaching a solution to a problem. Fourthly, Berlyne claims that much of Piaget's theory could be explained with reference to habit family hierarchies in which one set of reasoning is linked to another to form a more complex set so that, 'logical thinking is the result of an internal series of implicit responses which represent a situation which acts as a stimulus and ways of transforming these situations. (1962a:130)

Much research in the Soviet Union could be said to be within the S–R tradition; it is unfortunate that so little is freely available in translation. Following Pavlov Russian investigators have posited a 'second signal system' by which they mean the use of words as mediators. Once words can stand for overt responses chaining becomes possible and together with this the ability to deal with abstraction. Berlyne (1963) quotes an experiment, somewhat analagous to the Kendlers, in which young children performed differently from older children and the explanation offered was that the older children were using the second signal system whereas the younger ones were not. The equipment used in this study was a board on which was a red and a green light either or both of which could be illuminated. The child was given a rubber bulb to hold which he had to press, or not to press, in response to the light signal. Whenever a red light appeared the experimenter said 'press' and gradually the child would press when the red light appeared but before the experimenter had time to say anything. However, if he started saying 'press when the green light appears' the older children quickly adapted but the younger ones, aged about three, had great difficulty. The younger children appeared to be reacting directly to the red light, as in classical conditioning, whereas the older ones as it were 'told' themselves that they must press when a red light appeared or when the green light appeared.

Using the same apparatus Luria (1961) demonstrated the role of speech in the regulation of behaviour. In his experiments, the youngest children, aged about two, having been told to press when the light appeared, would start pressing at once and could not co-ordinate seeing the light and pressing the bulb. By about three and a half the children would press when the light came on but could not learn to press for one light and not for another, on the contrary they pressed whenever a light came on. By five or six the correct response appeared. Luria and his associates tried to get the children to use words as an aid to correct performance and found that even at age four words had an 'impelling' function but not a 'directing' one. The children were told to press twice when a light appeared and since up to age five or six they could not do this, Luria told them to say 'go, go' when the light appeared and they responded by correctly pressing twice. However, when they were told to say 'I shall press twice' they ceased to press twice but gave one long press. Luria concludes that the words 'go, go' were not acting as mediators so much as impelling the child to press. Luria argues that words have several distinct functions, firstly, an orientating function so that if the experimenter said 'fetch the ball' the child would look at the ball but not get it; secondly, an impulsive function as was exemplified in the 'go, go' example; thirdly, a selective function in that the child could learn to press the bulb when he saw the light and, finally, a pre-selective function so that at about the age of five, the child could be told 'press when the red light comes on, and don't press when the green light comes on' and performed correctly when the experiment began. Russian psychologists are also concerned with what they call the 'orientating response' or 'orientating reaction' by means of which the organism is alerted to the situation and by being alerted can make plans before engaging on a task. Berlyne comments that 'the interesting finding that emerges from those numerous [Russian] experiments is that verbal instruction and imitation are much more effective if they are directed towards orienting responses as well as executive responses. In other words, in teaching a child how to carry out a complex task, one must make sure that he is also taught how to organize his orienting response. (1963:180) This finding is in accord with that of the Americans, Shipman and Hess (see p. 130) and is obviously relevant for education.

Heinz Werner

Werner's theory is of interest not because it leads to neat experiments but because of his thorough-going development emphasis and the influence of his speculations on later writers. Firstly he sees man as representing a discontinuity with the animal world:

the developmental transformation from animal to human existence entails a radical change in the nature of the trans-

37

actions between the organism and its milieus: human beings are not merely, nor mainly, organisms reacting to stimuli or responding to things-of-action. Man . . . is directed towards knowing. The orientation toward, and the capacity for, knowing are essential and irreducible characteristics of man. (1963:12)

He defines developmental change as directed alteration which comes about through a dialectical process by means of which the organism originally makes differentiations and hence orders its environment, and subsequently hierarchically integrates these discrete differentiations. In this way the organism both changes yet keeps itself intact so that there is a form of continuity between primitive and mature thought:

whenever development occurs it proceeds from a state of relative globality and lack of differentiation to a state of increasing differentiation, articulation, and hierarchic integration. (1957:126)

Initially the environment affects the organism by physiochemical stimuli which cause it to react in stereo-typical ways. This stage is succeeded by one in which the organism orders the environment either by individually learned response patterns or behaviour specific to the species and therefore it becomes a field or fields of stimulus signs or signals which guide behaviour. Finally, the organism neither just reacts to nor organizes the environment but 'knows' it in 'the form of perceptualized or conceptualized objects' (1967:9). The emergence of symbolic behaviour is man's means of going beyond the responses of other species:

at the post-neonatal human level, with the emergence of a basic directiveness towards knowing, man's hand and man's brain participate in the construction of tangible tools out of the properties of the environment and the construction of cognitive objects (percepts and concepts) which mediate between man and his physical milieu: it is primarily towards these objects that man's distinctive behaviour is orientated. It is in this context, as we shall attempt to show, that the most significant of man's instrumentalities, *the symbol* is formed. (1967:10–11)

Thus through differentiation and integration man develops the means of representing his world by symbols, which range from images and gestures to words and mathematical notation and the ability to cognize experience via these means of representation.

An early study of his (1952) was designed to illustrate the developmental process as representing a shift from undifferentiated responses to those requiring differentiation and hierar-

38

chical organization. In this experiment children between the ages of nine and thirteen were asked to discover the meaning of non-sense words. Each word was used in six different sentences and the child was given each sentence in turn. At the end of each sentence he had to say what he thought the word meant and then change his interpretations if it did not seem to fit in with the next sentence. It was made clear that each word had only one meaning and that it could be used with this meaning in each of the sentences. For example:

You can't fill anything with a *contavish*
The more you take out of a *contavish* the larger it gets.
Before the house is finished the walls must have *contavishes*.
You can't hear or touch a *contavish*.
A bottle has only one *contavish*.
John fell in a *contavish* in the road.

Children of different ages exhibited more primitive or more advanced processes. The former were replaced by the latter, which were in their turn replaced by even more fully advanced responses, although the more primitive did not disappear entirely. For example, the youngest children, having chosen a meaning on hearing the first sentence could not change it when it did not fit in a subsequent sentence. All the children showed some rigidity but it was less apparent as age increased. The children had in fact to view each word as part of the sentence in which it appeared but capable of being removed from it and not bound to one meaning just because that meaning had previously been possible. To succeed the child had to differentiate the various possible meanings and out of these choose the one that fitted all cases. What they tended to do was use 'aggregation', 'pluralization', and 'transposition'. A child 'aggregating' put the several meanings he had found together and said the word meant '*a* plus *b*'. 'Pluralization' referred to solutions where a vague general meaning was given to the word. 'Transpositon' occurred when two words were used which the child claimed were 'kind'a like' each other, for example, 'burnt' and 'dirty'. Werner's emphasis on differentiation and integration through the use of symbols is in some ways reminiscent of mediational theories but his orientation is, in fact, closer to Jerome Bruner's, since both men stress the essentially human nature of cognitive processes.

Jerome Bruner

Jerome Bruner's approach to cognition is overridingly psychological. Piaget is, in fact, chiefly interested in knowledge.

Bruner, on the other hand, is concerned with the process of knowing, that is with how a person deals with information through selection, retention, and transformation. Bruner (1966) states his position very clearly when he says:

> We believe that intellectual growth can be understood only in terms of the psychological mechanisms that mediate it and that the explanation of growth cannot be affected by involving the nature of culture, the nature of language, the inherent logic of child thought, or the nature of man's evolutionary history. One finds no internal push to growth without a corresponding external pull, for, given the nature of man as a species, growth is as dependent upon a link with the external amplifiers of man's powers as it is upon those powers themselves. (1966:6)

He has, in his many works, been involved in studying the nature of man's powers, and the role of the 'external amplifiers', for example family and educational experiences. This dual concern has led him, unlike Piaget, to spell out the educational implications of his findings.

But his view is like Piaget's in that he thinks all knowing is a form of construction in which the knower plays an active part. Even the infants' world is conceived of as an inferential and constructed one since Bruner stresses the similarities, rather than the differences, between perception and cognition. The individual is thought to construct his perceptual world out of the information given by the senses. Likewise all skills are described as being the result of intentions, feedback, and structure. Perception is, firstly, a decision-making process in that the perceiver has to decide what it is he thinks he is seeing: is the dark shape in the shadows a fallen tree or a fellow human about to pounce? Secondly, the perceiver bases his decisions on certain cues which he gains from the object being perceived and which he orders in accordance with the schemes he has developed. Thirdly, on the basis of these cues he 'guesses' or 'infers', the nature of the object. 'Going from a cue to an inference of identity is probably the most ubiquitous and primitive cognitive activity'. (1973:19) Obviously such a process is a rudimentary form of categorization and perception therefore involves categorization in that it requires the perceiver to recognize certain attributes and on the basis of these attributes decide that an object is or is not a member of the hypothesized class. The degree to which a true identification is made, that is the extent to which the perception is 'veridical', will depend on the range of the perceiver's categories and his ability to utilize the category he has at his disposal.

The constructive nature of perception was demonstrated by Bruner (1947) in a series of experiments with ten-year-old children. When asked to judge the size of coins (by adjusting a circle of light to the apparent size of the coin they were being shown), all the children shown coins over-estimated their size, whereas a group of children shown grey discs instead of coins only made slight errors of estimation. Bruner argued that socially valued objects, coins, would be over-estimated in comparison with socially neutral objects like grey discs. Rich children showed less tendency to over-estimate the size of the coins than did poor children since, presumably, the poor children had a greater need of these valued objects. However, when the coins were removed and the children had to estimate their size from memory the rich children's tendency to over-estimate increased and the poor children's decreased. This result tied up with Bruner's view of memory: 'the most important thing about memory is not storage of past experience, but the retrieval of what is relevant in some usable form'. (1973:327) If memory is also a form of reconstruction it may be that the rich children in the memory condition were more inclined to fantasize whereas the poor children, although misled by their need when the coins were present, became more realistic when the coins were absent.

Bruner's individual approach to cognitive development is apparent in his treatment of simple skill (1971), for example lifting a barrier to obtain a toy or grasping an object. Skilled activity is deemed to have three components: firstly, intention, whereby the end state to be achieved is specified; secondly, the various activities necessary for achieving this end state have to be identified and ordered serially; and, thirdly, a form of feedback is employed which enables a particular sub-activity to be varied or abandoned altogether if the nature of the on-going activity makes it inappropriate. Intention is thus essential since it not only determines the end state but it enables the performer to monitor his behaviour and adapt it in the light of the original goal, so that what is *being* achieved can be compared with what is *to be* achieved and corrected if necessary. The arousal of intention has, for Bruner, similar qualities to the orientating response studied by the Soviet psychologists. The child's interest having been aroused he can then go into the serially ordered routines which will give him success. Put like this it is possible to see how Bruner is able to link skills with problem-solving and see skill learning as a form of activity which will later be further refined into the higher mental processes.

In perceptual and skilled activity the performer has, according to Bruner, to 'go beyond the information given' and this aspect of human knowing is even more apparent with respect to cognition. What, exactly, does this mean? Classification requires the person to treat the incoming stimuli in a certain way. To recognize a stick as a stick and not a snake presupposes the ability to recognize the defining attributes of each and hence correctly identify the stick as a member of the class 'stick' and exclude it from the class 'snake'. To make more subtle distinctions such as those between grass snakes and adders requires the individual to possess the appropriate categories. To illustrate this activity Bruner quotes William James's remark (1890) that the beginning of cognitive life is signalled by the ability to say 'hello! thingumbob again'. (Bruner, 1973:219). A coding system is defined as 'a set of contingently related non-specific categories. It is a person's manner of grouping and relating information about his world and is constantly subject to change and reorganization.' (1973:222) The way an organism behaves enables the experimenter to infer the coding system being used. For example, if a rat learns to find its way through a maze by choosing a left/right, left/right pattern and it then learns its way through a second maze which requires a right/left, right/left pattern more quickly than a rat who had not learned the first maze, one can infer that it has 'coded', or internalized, a strategy that tells it to take alternate paths. Bruner, in a further refinement of the maze learning experiment, had the pairs of paths painted black or white (direction was not important). When the rat chose a white, then a black, then a white, and then a black path, Bruner was able to infer that the rat had coded alternation in general and not just left/right alternation.

In an experiment with adults, human subjects, who were matured speakers of Swedish, French, Dutch and English, were asked to reproduce random strings of letters and strings which could have existed in their native language. In handling the random strings the subjects did not differ but they did show considerably greater facility at handling nonsense-strings that were like their own language as compared with similar strings in another language. To take Bruner's example, it is relatively easy to sense the language from which each of the following nonsense words were constructed: 'majölkkor, klook, gerlanch, otivanche, trianode, fattoloni'. Bruner concludes 'when one learns a language one learns a coding system that goes beyond words'. (1973:224)

Perception, skill, and learning in terms of utilizing codes are all related to cognitive growth but perhaps Bruner is best known for his views on the nature of this growth. Growth is seen as a development of two forms of competence. Firstly, the ability to 'represent the recurrent regularities of the environment' (1973:348) and, secondly, the ability to transcend the momentary by developing ways of linking past to present and to future. These two processes of representation and integration are the core of cognition. Where Piaget speaks of stages, for example, the sensori-motor or the 'operational', Bruner distinguishes three forms of representation, firstly 'enactive', secondly, 'iconic', and thirdly, 'symbolic'. Cognitive development is described as the development of these ways of representing the world.

Enactive representation appears first and is 'a mode of representing past events through appropriate motor responses' (1973:328). Its origins are to be found in the 'infant's need' to relate his action to his visual field. Initially, the child cannot separate his notion of the object from his actions towards it, in other words the child's rattle is not conceived of as separable from the action of shaking it so that if the rattle is dropped the infant continues to make shaking movements presumably in the hope that this will make the rattle exist in his hands again.

Iconic representation appears when the child is able to replace the action with an image or spatial scheme. Images are said to 'stand for' the object in the sense that a picture or map 'stands for' the object pictured. Iconic representation does not go beyond the perceptually salient and is not helpful in forming concepts but, nevertheless, it is a way of representing the world and may be facilitative of certain tasks. Kuhlman (1960) found that junior school children who were imagers were superior to non-imagers in tasks which required them to learn to relate arbitrary verbal labels to pictures but inferior at the conceptual task of recognizing what a set of pictures had in common.

Symbolic representation is the last form to develop and is the most adaptable and flexible. An image is tied to that which it represents whereas a symbol, such as a word, has a purely arbitrary connection with the thing symbolized. Two basic features of symbolic representation are category and hierarchy so that the user of a symbolic form is able to order his world through symbols, and thus be freed from the constraints of both his own actions towards objects and the nature of his images. The child at this stage therefore has moved from 'doing' through 'sensing' to 'symbolizing.'

The transition from iconic to symbolic representation was demonstrated in an experiment by Bruner and Kenny (1966). In this experiment children between the ages of five and seven were shown an array of glasses which varied both in diameter and height (fig. 2.3). The children were asked, firstly, to replace a few glasses removed by the experimenters; secondly, to describe how the glasses were alike and how they differed; thirdly to remake the matrix after the glasses had been scrambled; and, finally, to remake the matrix when the experimenters had removed the glasses and replaced one in a different position – that is the glass that was previously in the bottom left hand corner was replaced in the top right hand corner. The final task was the critical one. All the

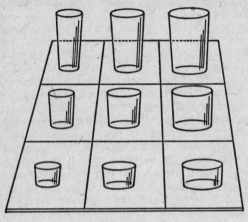

О 2 4 6 Scale in inches

(Bruner, 1973: 331)

Fig. 2.3 *Array of glasses used in study of matrix ordering*

children succeeded with the first and third tasks but in the final transposition task the seven-year-olds succeeded but the five-year-olds seemed 'to be dominated by an image of the original matrix (1973:332) and could not reorientate themselves sufficiently to carry out the task. A child using an iconic mode is therefore able to reproduce but not to restructure. The children's description of the glasses could be divided into 'dimensional', for example 'that one is higher and that one is shorter'; 'global', 'that one is bigger and that one is little'; and 'confounded', 'that one is tall and that one is little'. Their language use as expressed in the second part of the task was not related to performance on the untransposed matrix but confounded responses were associated with a poor performance on the transposition task.

The importance of conflict between the different modes of representation and the significance of language are important questions for Bruner. In a training experiment by Sonstroem (1966) the facilitating effect of conflict between the modes of representation was shown. Here six and seven-year-olds were tested and those who could not conserve substance (see p. 19) were divided into four groups: the first group reshaped the ball of clay themselves and had to say what the new shape was, they therefore both labelled and manipulated the clay. A second group saw the clay altered by the experimenter and were asked to name

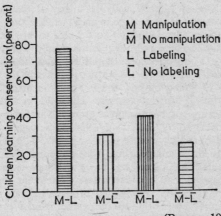

(Bruner, 1973: 322)

Fig. 2.4 *Per cent of children learning conservation with labelling and manipulation variables combined*

the shape; in this condition there was labelling without manipulation. The third group manipulated the clay but did not label; and the fourth group did neither. All the children were then tested again to see if the training sessions had improved their ability to conserve. The results showed that only when both manipulation and labelling were present were the post test scores markedly different (fig. 2.4). Bruner explained these results by saying that non-conservation was characteristic of children using the iconic mode who were dominated by appearance. When these children had to both manipulate and label, the enactive and symbolic modes were involved and together they conflicted with the iconic interpretation that a change in appearance represented a change in shape. Thus growth involves the development of various ways of representing the world and through the conflict between these representations further growth is stimulated.

Since the symbolic mode of representation is seen as the most advanced and since language is a major form of symbolizing it is not surprising that Bruner thinks that language is a more important determinant of cognitive development than does Piaget. Bruner's argument is that if the person can use language to encode stimuli this frees him from the world of appearances and gives greater stability, yet flexibility, to his cognition, provided that the linguistic labels are appropriate to the task and do offer a way of encoding relevant information. Language as well as being a system of labels is hierarchically organized. It has superordinate words like colour or shape. These may facilitate the development of the concepts they embody. To be able to use symbols frees the user from the here and now, that is from the present context.

Language is only one aspect of culture, even though an important one, and it is a person's culture that transmits to him the techniques of 'going beyond the information given' which, for Bruner, are at the heart of cognition. His ideas on the relationship between culture and cognition are often illustrated by a series of studies carried out by Greenfield (1966) in Senegal on the ability of children to conserve or to form concepts. The children were divided into three groups, those who attended no school, those who attended a bush school, and those who attended a city school. When given the classic conservation experiment involving the beakers (see p. 19) the unschooled children's ability to conserve or not conserve was as one would predict from Western studies but it was in their explanations, or what they considered constituted an explanation, that the clearest differences were seen. Firstly, when asked why they thought the tall beaker had more juice the reply would be 'because you poured it' thus endowing the experimenter with magical powers. After seven months of schooling these types of magical responses had entirely died out and as Bruner says: 'schools seem to promote the selfconsciousness born of a distinction between human processes and physical phenomena'. (1973:375) Secondly, the 'unschooled' children could not reply when asked 'why do you say . . .?', and could only reply when the question was rephrased as 'why is X true?'. It was as if they could not separate themselves and their statements about an event from the event itself. The schooled children however had learnt this form of selfconsciousness. For Bruner school is the agent of the culture and through schooling the child learns to selfconsciously evaluate his own statements and to use context-free linguistic symbols whereby he learns that words are arbitrary labels and not properties of objects. Hence schooling is of considerable interest to Bruner.

46

If cognitive growth is the result both of an internal push and an external pull and if it can be conceptualized as the development of the three modes of representation and their integration then certain implications for schooling follow. Firstly, the skills involved in manipulating and handling the environment, in perceiving and imagining, and in symbolically representing it should be developed to their greatest extent. Secondly, these skills can be taught in some form to children of any age but as they develop and their mastery increases then they will need to return to the skills but on a higher level, hence Bruner's image of 'the spiral curriculum' which was thought preferable to images of ladders or courses to be run. Thirdly, instruction should be related to the mode of representation used by the child but growth encouraged by bringing the other modes to bear on the same problem. Finally, teaching should be concerned with structure not facts alone so that the child is primarily engaged in learning how to know.

3
Perceptual development

Perception and cognition

Traditionally perceptual and conceptual processes have been distinguished and there are in fact good reasons for this. Piaget (1969) considers fourteen ways in which perception differs from intelligence but admits that the most fundamental problem in the study of intelligence is the extent to which it is derived from perceptual experience. He stresses the immediate here and now nature of perceptions and their role, in that perceptions, while they cannot be the source of knowledge, since knowledge requires the application of the operative schemes (see page 16) can nevertheless act as a means of connecting actions and operations with objects and events:

> In the end, the relative adequacy of any perception to any object depends on a constructive process and not on an immediate contact. During this constructive process the subject tries to make use of whatever information he has, incomplete, deformed, or false as it may be, and to build it into a system which corresponds as nearly as possible to the properties of the objects. He can only do this by a method which is both cumulative and corrective. (Piaget, 1969:365)

It is therefore necessary to consider both the perceptual and conceptual aspects of any cognitive act and it is thus appropriate to consider perceptual development as a necessary component in the understanding of cognitive development. A person's thinking is influenced by his perception and what he perceives is to a greater or lesser extent influenced by what he thinks.

48

The extent to which the one influences or is influenced by the other forms the basis of the 'nativist' versus the 'empiricist' argument which, although as much philosophical as psychological, is important because it occurs in other areas of psychology in different guises. In language acquisition (see page 97) the problem is posed in terms of whether children have an 'innate' knowledge of, for example, grammatical relations or whether language is 'learned' by imitating adults. In studies of intelligence the 'nature/nurture' controversy is fundamentally on whether 'intelligence', if defined as facility in processing certain types of data, is the result of a person's heredity or the environment in which he has been reared. In considering perception the nativists argue that what we see is influenced by innate factors and is independent of experience whereas the empiricists maintain that, initially, the mind is a blank, with no innate preconceptions, so that all perception is based on previous experience. We have, if the empiricists are right, in a sense to learn to see, whereas if the nativists are, we initially see what we expect to see or our perceptions are governed by innate predispositions rather than previous experience. The nativists would therefore link perception more closely to cognition than the empiricists although of course cognitive capacities must be involved in using experience as a basis for subsequent perception.

It can be argued that the primary perceptual experience is merely the reception of a sensation. The senses are stimulated by a sight, sound, touch, taste or smell. It is at a subsequent, secondary, stage that this initial stimulation is perceived as 'an X'. If this separation is made then cognition enters very early into perception and the perceptual act becomes little more than the initial reception and recording of stimuli. Bruner (1957) states that 'perception involves an act of categorization' (1973:7) and distinguishes between 'the sensory stuff from which percepts are made' (1973:7) and the use of cues in inferring the categorical identity of a perceived object, both of which he sees as 'features of perception'. He is therefore claiming that similar processes of inference are applied in both perceptual and conceptual activities. The process is a categorizing process so that:

under any conditions of perception, what is achieved by the perceiver is the categorization of an object or sensory event in terms of more or less abundant or reliable cues. Representation consists in knowing how to utilize cues with reference to a system of categories. It also depends upon the creation of a system of categories-in-relationship that fit the nature of the world in which the person must live. In fine, adequate perceptual representation involves the learning of appropriate categories, the learning of cues useful in placing objects appropriately in such systems of categories, and the learning of what objects are likely to occur in the environment. (1973:12)

This is not to say that perception and cognition are identical but rather to stress the constructive nature of both perception and cognition and the significance of both as cognitive processes.

Perception, however, can be taken to mean both a reception of, and a response to, stimuli provided that all the information needed for the response is present at the time. Wohlwill argues in a similar way: 'if we ask ourselves how one might operationally distinguish between a purely perceptual and a purely inferential task, one criterion for inference would be the opportunity for the subject to supplement or replace the sensory data with information or knowledge not contained in the immediate stimulus field.' (1962:98) The nativist position is therefore strengthened whenever an infant responds to a perceptual stimuli in a way which it has had no opportunity of learning. Perception and conception are best seen as two ends of the continuum of cognitive development. Perception is a basic cognitive process, that is, it is a necessary condition for subsequent development. An infant must receive some sensory stimulation for without it its cognitive development would be abnormal, although it can compensate for deficiency in one modality, for example, hearing. At the perceptual end conceptual elements may be present, and at the conceptual end perceptual elements are necessary, but the emphasis placed on the one or the other process differs depending on the stage of development attained.

Wohlwill (1962) distinguishes three dimensions for relating perception and cognition: redundancy (excess information), selectivity, and contiguity. At the perceptual level redundancy is high and it decreases as conceptual thinking increases, so that when symbolic notation is used in mathematics or logic there is no redundancy at all. Irrelevant information, on the other hand, is less distracting at the conceptual than the perceptual level since the more mature thinker is able, through his concepts, to select the salient and ignore the rest. For example, once a person has the concept of invariance, perceptual changes such as the length of a line of coins or the height of liquid in a beaker will be ignored as irrelevant. At the perceptual level separate pieces of information can only be used together if they are near in time or space, whereas at the conceptual level contiguity is not so important since symbolic mediation enables a person to relate two or more pieces of information even though they are temporarily or spatially apart.

Wohlwill performed a simple, but elegant experiment to test the significance of the redundancy and selectivity dimensions. The subjects' task was to pick out the odd one from a set of three geometric figures. These figures were presented on five sheets which differed in terms of the redundant and/or irrelevant information they contained. Four attributes were varied: shape,

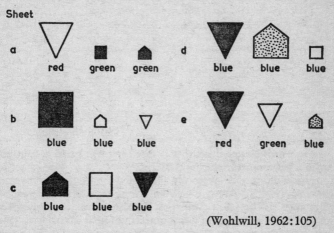

(Wohlwill, 1962:105)

Fig. 3.1 *Sample stimulus sets used to represent different amounts of redundant and irrelevant information*

colour, shading and size (fig. 3.1) and the hypothesis was that 'as relevant information decreased or irrelevant information increased, there would be a gradual shift from a perceptual mode to a conceptual mode of functioning, reflected in three different ways. In children errors would increase, and younger subjects would show a greater effect in this respect than older subjects; for adults the time taken to complete each sheet would be directly related to the degree of irrelevant or redundant information.' (1962:106) The results confirmed the hypothesis (Table 3.A, p.52).

The role of experiment

In all studies of human behaviour speculation is only valuable in so far as it can be tested empirically. What is required is imaginative thinking followed by ingenious experimentation. Perception is a particularly difficult area since perception is an internal process and the experimenter has to make inferences on the basis of the behaviour he observes. But he has to be sure, firstly, that what the subject perceives is what the experimenter thinks he is perceiving; secondly, that the subject's behaviour is the result of his perceptual activity alone and not, for example, of his memory; and, thirdly, that the subject will view the task in the same way

Table 3.A Mean number of errors and mean time (for adults) per sheet.

Sheet	MEAN NUMBER OF ERRORS			Mean Time (Adults)
	3rd Grade	5th Grade	Adults	
a	·6	·5	·1	17·0 sec.
b	·8	·3	·4	19·8
c	1·2	1·2	·4	19·5
d	3·4	3·0	1·2	32·2
e	3·8	3·9	1·9	31·0

(Wohlwill, 1962:106)

as the experimenter does, that is that they will be in agreement as to what the nature of the task is.

These difficulties are nicely illustrated by Bower (1974) and Bryant (1974). There is a well known perceptual illusion called the 'auto kinetic effect', whereby if the observer is placed in a dark room in which there is just one spot of light this spot of light will appear to move as much as forty degrees although it is in fact stationary. Various explanations have been suggested and have been found wanting but one very important fact was being overlooked and that was that normally the observer is 'represented on his own retina' (Bower, 1974:50). Bower quotes Gibson's (1950) observation that the observer actually sees a portion of his nose under normal viewing conditions – this, of course, is not apparent unless one eye is shut. Now, if part of the nose is within the observer's visual field it would form a fixed point to which all other judgements of position could be referred. However, once the observer is in darkness this frame of reference is removed and he, literally, becomes invisible to himself.

Under normal conditions of illumination an observer, asked to judge the position of an object relative to himself, can see both the object and himself. By contrast, under conditions where position perception breaks down – conditions of darkness with luminous objects – the observer can only see the objects. We would not expect an observer to locate the position of an invisible object relative to himself. Likewise, we should not

52

expect an observer to be able to locate the position of an object relative to himself when he is himself invisible. (1974:51)

Once it is realized that the observer's view of himself is an essential element in the perception of position, effects like the auto kinetic become easily explicable; but a failure to take this aspect into account makes such effects difficult to explain.

The significance of memory is raised by Bryant (1974) when he points out that in classical transitivity tasks the child may fail not because he is unable to make inferences but because he cannot remember the information which he requires to form the basis of his inferences. One classic transitivity task involves showing a child two sticks, *a* and *b*, such that *a* is longer than *b*. He is then shown stick *b* plus another stick *c* which is shorter than *b*. Thus *a* is longer than *b* and *b* is longer than *c*. The child is then asked whether *a* or *c* is longer. If the child fails it is assumed that he cannot make the necessary inference whereas Bryant points out that the problem could be that he has forgotten which stick in the previously presented pairs, that is *a* and *b*, is the longer. There is another problem associated with this experiment and that is that when the child does give the correct answer he may do so for the wrong reason; since if he has only been presented with two sets of pairs he may merely parrot the label he has associated with *a* and *c* when first shown them, that is, that *a* is long and *c* is short; he may therefore repeat that *c* is shorter not because he has worked out that it has to be but because he has associated the label 'shorter' with the stick *c*.

Bryant repeated this experiment and attempted to control these factors. To resolve the memory problem he made certain that the child could remember the initial data before asking him to make the inference. Secondly, by including more sets so that *a* was compared with *b*, *b* with *c*, *c* with *d*, and *d* with *e*, the child could not parrot a particular length when asked to compare *b* to *d* since both *b* and *d* had been the longer stick in one comparison and the shorter in the other. When Bryant performed this experiment he found that children could make a successful inference and argues:

Two main points follow from this conclusion. The first is that Piaget's theory about logical development must, to some extent, be wrong. His experiments did not ensure that children could remember the comparisons which they were asked to combine inferentially, and it now seems clear that children can manage this sort of inference provided that they can remember the information on which the inference has to be based. The second point is that this evidence shows that children have the logical mechanism for using framework cues as a basis for organizing and categorizing their perceptual experience through perceptual inferences. (1974:48)

However, to be quite certain that children have mastered the question of necessity – that is if *a* is greater than *b* and *b* greater than *c*, *a must* be greater than *c* – it would be necessary to test the children who had mastered the *b/d* inference on another similar task to ensure that they had indeed developed the notion of inference and were not just responding to what they perceived as the qualities of a specific array. Admittedly, with the materials presented by Bryant, the children apparently made inferences, but evidence of their ability to generalize this is necessary before one could claim that they had developed an inferential 'scheme'. Bryant's arguments do however demonstrate the importance of taking all aspects of the task into account before drawing conclusions.

Bryant also illustrates the confusion that can arise when child and experimenter, although ostensibly engaged on the same task, perceived its nature differently. He takes as an example another classic experiment, namely the one to test number invariance. The usual procedure is to show the child two rows of counters laid out so that there is a one to one correspondence between the counters, and to ask the child if there are the same number of counters in each row. If he agrees that there are, one row is spread out and therefore it appears longer. The question is then repeated. The child will usually say that the row which is longer has more counters and this is taken as evidence that the child has not developed the concept of invariance, whereby, if nothing is added and nothing taken away, the numbers must remain the same. The child is judged to have been misled by the perceptual appearance of the longer line. Bryant makes the intriguing suggestion that the child may be using two types of cue to judge number; one being one to one correspondence and the other being length of line. Thus when the child sees the lengthened line he is not saying that the number of counters has increased but judging his former statement to be mistaken. The child could in fact be implying that he thought they were the same but now he has looked again he realizes that his first judgement was in error. The child, in fact, experiences a conflict between two judgements.

Bryant tested the conflict hypothesis in a series of experiments, one of which was based on the fact that given the three displays A, B, C (fig. 3.2) children are consistently correct with A, consistently incorrect with B, and respond at random with C, since C cannot be solved by using either the one to one or the length method of judging. If, however, the child is shown display A first and it is then transformed into C, if he understands the principle of invariance, he should be able to answer correctly for C since he does not use a method of judging length in C which is in conflict with his method for A. Given that his answers to C were

Invariance

A (above chance) B(below chance) C (chance)

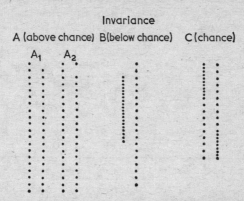

Fig. 3.2 *Counter display*

random, when it was presented in isolation, any improvement would show that he had used the information concerning the relative numbers in the two rows, which he gained by seeing the A display despite the perceptual re-ordering. He would, therefore, be displaying some understanding of invariance. Bryant performed an experiment with four groups of children aged three, four, five and six. There were three sessions for each group; in the first the displays were presented and the children were asked which line had more counters. In the second, the experimental session, A was transformed into B, and A was transformed into C. In the final session they were again shown the displays. It was the experimental session that was crucial, and this showed that when A was transformed into B their responses were as erroneous as in the first session, that is the longer line was judged to have more counters. But their responses to C improved dramatically when they saw it transformed from A (Table 3.B). Bryant concludes:

It seems then that children could transfer the relative information about which row was the more numerous across a transformation to a display which would not on its own have produced a correct judgement. So they must be able to understand that the perceptual transformation has not actually altered the

55

Table 3.B Mean Scores on A, B, and C displays (A–B, A–C)

			Pre-test	Exp. session	Post-test
	A	$\bar{x}$	7·13		7·40
		SD	0·88		0·88
Three-year group	B	$\bar{x}$	1·40	0·90	0·80
		SD	2·06	1·26	1·38
	C	$\bar{x}$	4·10	6·70	3·50
		SD	1·26	1·53	1·45
	A	$\bar{x}$	7·07		7·33
		SD	1·06		0·69
Four-year group	B	$\bar{x}$	1·60	1·20	1·70
		SD	1·82	1·83	1·73
	C	$\bar{x}$	3·40	7·00	4·10
		SD	1·93	0·97	1·37
	A	$\bar{x}$	7·27		7·40
		SD	0·68		0·31
Five-year group	B	$\bar{x}$	0·66	1·53	0·53
		SD	1·30	1·22	1·02
	C	$\bar{x}$	4·40	6·53	3·80
		SD	1·89	1·09	1·25
	A	$\bar{x}$	7·33		7·47
		SD	0·69		0·72
Six-year group	B	$\bar{x}$	0·87	1·27	1·20
		SD	1·75	2·14	1·68
	C	$\bar{x}$	4·20	7·27	3·67
		SD	1·45	1·06	1·40

(Exp. session scores are for B or C after transformation from A.)
(Bryant, 1974: 137)

numbers of counters involved. Children only fail to transfer information across the transformation when the first and second judgement are in conflict with another. (1974: 138)

These experiments have been described in detail to show that experimentation is crucial, to our understanding of perceptual and conceptual development and of the interaction between the two, but that unless the experiments are very carefully controlled the information they appear to give may be at best incomplete and at worst positively misleading.

Perception studies can be divided into those which are primarily descriptive and those which are primarily explanatory. This is not to say that any experiment is totally devoid of either explanation or description but the former seek to describe what is happening when we perceive whereas the latter concentrate on a particular hypothesis and test it in detail. Descriptive studies often produce evidence for perceptual development between birth and adulthood and explanatory studies can build on these by taking one particular change and attempting to isolate the mechanism, or mechanisms, responsible, in other words one group is primarily concerned with what happens and the other with how and why it happens.

Zaporozhets (1965) together with other members of his laboratory in the USSR tested the hypothesis that when a child perceives he is both exploring the object and correcting his impression of it. He believes that at birth the infant has a form of 'orientating response' which means that it will look towards stimuli, continue looking at them, and watch their movements. These early responses, however, are limited to looking at rather than exploring the object. He found that young children aged three to four and a half, when asked to recognize objects by touching but not looking at them, did not explore the objects systematically but played with them by pushing and shaking and attempted to find out what they were through these actions. Older children aged six to seven and a half however did explore the objects systematically by touching their contours to find out their shape, weighing them in their hands, etc. When the children were filmed looking at new objects, similar age differences were found. The children were asked to look carefully at figures projected on a screen so that they would be able to recognize them again; three to four-year-olds did not follow the contours or scan the object, rather they concentrated on certain portions, often the centre, and made many mistakes when asked to pick out the object they had seen from an array. Four to five-year-olds spent less time looking at any one point, made more eye movements and appeared to be noting the length of the object, they did not follow the contours but were more successful at picking the objects out. Five- and six-year-olds did begin by tracing the outline but then fixated a particularly salient feature. It was not until six to seven that the children carefully looked at the outline of the figure and achieved one hundred per cent success in the recognition test. These results supported Klein's (1963) earlier finding that when asked to match objects which they had only been allowed to touch younger children matched on the basis of texture rather than on the basis of shape and that the younger children did not explore the contours of objects.

Having observed this developmental progression the experimenters set out to find its causes. They, therefore, let children learn about new objects in four ways, by looking only, touching only, looking and touching, and playing with them by having to put them into matching shaped holes in a board. The three to four-year-olds were much better at recognizing the objects with which they had played when they were presented together with other objects. Zaporozhets concluded that such practical activity was conducive to forming a 'perceptive image' of the object. Looking or touch were not enough, the child had to be able to *use* the object in some way before he could perceive it, or, perhaps, before he could remember it well enough to pick it out from an array. Thus experience of an object in the environment could be an important way in which children begin to appreciate the properties of objects and they subsequently learn how to take in important features more quickly and efficiently. Perception is here seen as an activity which involves building up information on the basis of previous experience.

Potter argues in a similar way that 'two major phases are distinguishable in an act of perceptual recognition: first, organizing the incoming stimuli into figure and background, texture, tridimensionality, and the like; and second, relating this organized perception to one or more categories – recognition itself.' (1966:103) To test this she showed a series of six pictures, each of which was initially out of focus and gradually became more clearly in focus, to groups ranging in age from three to twenty. The subjects' comments while they looked at the picture and attempted to recognize it were recorded. The results showed that the ability to integrate information correctly increased with age, thus the four-year-old was only able to see one thing at a time and was not able to make use of guesses he had made before; the five-year-old was able to break the picture down but could not build it up again, whereas the nine-year-old was able to generate hypotheses that were appropriate to the picture and distinguish them from those that were not. The adult would make inferences, check hypotheses, and make use of all the information he had obtained whilst looking at the series.

Both the Russian and American experiments, therefore suggest that development means a greater efficiency at obtaining information and a greater ability to make use of the information obtained. Experiments of this kind are informative in showing age changes but others have revealed that young children can perform discrimination tasks provided that the array is small and the objects attractive. Bryant (1974) devised an experiment based on the observation that babies are interested in and will reach for objects that make a noise. He used two pairs of objects and showed each infant only one of the pairs. (fig. 3.3). Firstly, the

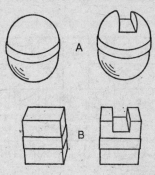

(Bryant, 1974:163)

Fig. 3.3 *Shapes used in matching task*

infant was shown the objects which were placed on a table in front of him but out of reach. The objects were then both removed. Secondly, one was returned to the table and was made to make a noise, before it was removed. Thirdly, both objects were replaced on the table and the experimenters recorded which objects the infant reached for. He found that with infants under twelve months twenty three out of thirty given pair A and twenty two out of thirty given pair B first reached for the noisy object thereby showing that they could discriminate.

A variation of this experiment showed that the infants were able to use tactile information better than had been thought previously. This second experiment was the same as the first except that in the second stage the experimenter, keeping her hand over the object, put the infant's hand on it and then her hand over the infant's, it was then that the object made a noise. In the final stage twenty three out of thirty infants given pair A reached for the noisy object, but only nineteen out of thirty given pair B. Therefore, with respect to pair A, the infants were able to discriminate by touch and make use of this information when they subsequently saw the object.

In addition to showing what an infant can do and showing how less mature perceivers differ from the more mature, experimenters have looked at the type of errors made by children of different ages. Gibson was concerned with the specific question of children's ability to discriminate letter-like forms which has an obvious relevance to skills such as reading since if the child is perceptually unable to discriminate *b* from *d* or *p* from *q* then he is unlikely to master a complex task which requires this more

Fig. 3.4 *Artificial graphic forms and twelve variants*

Standard	L to C 1	L to C 2	L to C 3	45° R	90° R	R-L Rev.	U-D Rev.	180° R	Perspective trs! Slant L	Tilt back	Close	Break

(Gibson, 1963:17)

simple discrimination before he can even begin. For her experiment a series of twelve letter-like forms were made and then twelve variants were made of the original twelve standard forms; these consisted in 'three degrees of transformations of line to curve or curve to line: five transformations of rotation or reversal, two perspective transformations (slant left and tilt back): and two topological changes, a break and a close' (1963:17) (fig. 3.4). The children, aged between four and eight, were then shown a Standard Card and the twelve variants together with an exact copy of the Standard. These thirteen cards were laid out in a line below the original Standard and the children were asked to pick out the one which matched the original Standard. She found that

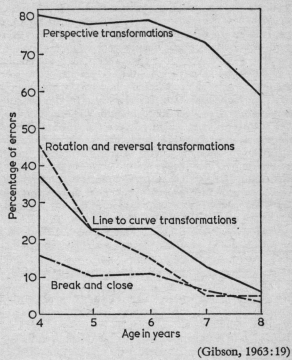

(Gibson, 1963:19)

Fig. 3.5 *Errors in matching variants with standard graphic forms by type of variant and age of S*

all errors decreased with age but that some types of error, for example perspective transformation, was still very common even at age eight (fig. 3.5).

Infant perception

Despite the difficulty of studying infants some of the most illuminating perceptual experiments have used infants as subjects and since conceptual activities appear to be to some extent based on the perceptual world of the infant the nature of this world is of considerable interest. Three comparatively early experiments (Fantz, 1961 and 1966; Gibson, 1963) were concerned with what the infant perceived and have stimulated a considerable number of subsequent studies.

Fantz (1961) was concerned with the extent to which the infant was able to perceive distinct forms and differentiate between them. As a measure of whether the infant could perceive a form he recorded the activity of the infant's eyes arguing that if the infant looked at some forms more than others such selectivity must imply the ability to see them as distinct. Infants between one and fifteen weeks were shown pairs of stimuli and the amount of time they spent looking at each was recorded. In all cases the most complex pairs were given more attention (fig. 3.6).

He then considered whether, given that infants could distinguish forms, some formal configurations would be more attractive than others because they were salient features of the infants' environment. Human beings are important to the human infant, and therefore if they did show preferences these preferences might be expected to be with respect to the human face. Accordingly, the infants were shown three head-shaped discs, one of which had a face painted on it, one had a scrambled face, and one, the control, was painted black where the hair might be with the rest left blank. The infants tested were age between four days and five months but the results were the same for all age levels, namely, that the infants looked most at the realistic face, less at the scrambled face, and took no notice of the control. A third experiment showed that when given a choice between coloured and patterned surfaces the patterns, in particular the face, were consistently looked at longer than the coloured discs.

Fantz (1966) maintained that although it had been thought that perceptual activity was dependent on previous motor activity of the eyes, hands, and indeed the whole body, his view was that it was the perceptual experience that preceded, and was a necessary condition for, the development of motor behaviour directed by vision. Given that infants show a preference for patterns, Fantz then tested the degree to which they would respond to a new pattern, thereby showing that they were able to recognize patterns they had seen before, and therefore perceived the new one as one which had not been seen before. He did this by taking eleven complex pictures and showing them to the infants in pairs. One of the pair was always the same picture, but it was paired each time with a different one. Infants aged six to eight weeks looked at the familiar and new pictures approximately equally, but infants aged two to six months looked more at the new one. The ability of the infants to know what is new means that, whilst still inactive, they are able to prepare for subsequent active exploration of the environment. Fantz concludes:

> While it may not be true that the eyes are a window to the soul, it is true that the direction of gaze as reflected in the eyes of the

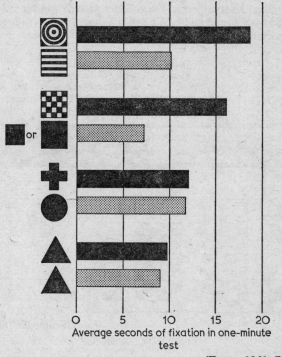

Average seconds of fixation in one-minute test

(Fantz, 1961: 70)

Fig. 3.6 *Interest in form*

infant can be a window to his perceptual and mental processes if one is patient enough to wait until the window is opened, and if adequate conditions of observations are obtained. It has not been possible to see inside clearly enough to know whether there is a manikin looking out at the observer: but the findings to date have tended to destroy other myths – that the world

63

of the neonate is a big booming confusion, that his visual field is a form of blur, that his mind is a blank state, that his brain is decorticate, and that his behaviour is limited to reflexes or undirected mass movements. The infant sees a patterned and organized world which he explores discriminatingly within the limited means at his command. (1966: 171–2)

Gibson (1963) looked at infants' perception of space which she tested by the 'visual cliff'. This consisted of a glass top table with raised edges. Immediately underneath one half of the glass was a checked pattern whereas the checked pattern was on the floor beneath the second half of the glass. Thus, although the top felt solid, it looked as if there was a drop in the middle, since putting

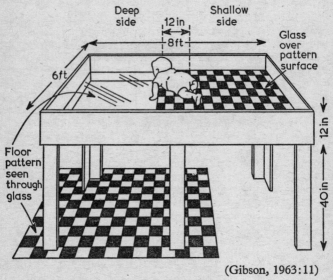

(Gibson, 1963:11)

Fig. 3.7 *The visual cliff*

the checks on the floor gave an impression of depth (fig. 3.7). The infant was then placed on the shallow side and invited, by being called by its mother or offered toys, to crawl over the 'deep' part. The majority of the infants, aged six and a half to twelve months, refused.

These early experiments showed that the infant was able to perceive aspects of his environment before he had had a great deal of experience in that environment. Recently, however, techniques have improved and it has become possible to make considerably more subtle tests. Given that the infant has some spatial sense in that he can perceive a drop, is he also able to locate objects and sounds in the space that surrounds him, that is can he tell right from left and both from straight ahead?

Bower (1974) argues that experimental results suggest that the notion of right, left and straight ahead are present before any learning could have occurred, but that the ability to pinpoint exactly where an object or sound is located seems to develop in infancy. The experiments he cites are those of Wertheimer (1962) and Bower and Wishart (1973). Wertheimer's subject was a new-born baby under ten minutes old. As soon as the baby was delivered a series of sounds were made to its right or left in random sequence. The baby looked in the correct direction for each sound thus showing that he could tell both left from right and had sufficient co-ordination and control to turn left and right as required. Gesell (1934) had said that until the age of five months visual orientation to a left or right sound was inaccurate. Bower and Wishart looked to see whether Gesell's finding was the result of poor visual or poor auditory location. That is, was it the case that the infant looked in the wrong place because he heard the sound in the wrong place, or heard the sound accurately but was unable to co-ordinate visually and therefore not able to look exactly where he had heard the sound? They therefore tested the same infants in two experimental conditions. In the first, the infants, in a lighted room, were shown an object either straight ahead or thirty degrees to the right or left. They were able to reach and hit the object and the number of times they succeeded in doing so was taken as a measure of the accuracy of their visual/motor co-ordination. The second condition was the same except that the infants were in the dark and the object made a noise, again the number of times the infant hit the object was taken as evidence of auditory/motor co-ordination. The results showed considerably greater visual accuracy.

If infants can locate objects in space can they perceive distance and can they notice that an object has moved? Fantz had shown that infants will look longer at a new stimulus. Following up this observation McKenzie and Day (1972) found that if the same object was shown ten times in one position and then the distance was changed the infant looked longer the eleventh time and they therefore concluded that the infant could perceive distance. Bower (1974), however, maintained that it might not be the distance as such that was being perceived but the fact that if the object moved further away it became smaller and if nearer bigger, and that it was the size change which was responsible for the infant's increased interest. He said:

> There are three main problem areas that concern us when we study the perception of distance in infants. The first is: Do infants perceive distance at all, or do they simply perceive the variables that specify distance? When presented with an approaching object, do they see the object approach (perception of distance, or do they simply see it expand (perception of the specifying variables)?. The second problem area is: When and how do infants succeed in correlating perception and action to produce accurate behaviour in space?. Thirdly, once these two are correlated, how does the organism adjust to growth within the components? (1974:18)

Bower himself had found (1971) that infants in their second week would make defensive movements when an object approached them in such a way that it looked as if it would hit them. He used this defensive reaction to test whether, in fact, they did perceive distances as such. In this experiment the infants were shown two objects, one after the other, the first was small and approached to within eight centimetres of the infants' face, the second was large and approached to within twenty centimetres. At these distances the object would appear to be the same size; therefore if the infants' were responding merely to the image of the object both would seem equally dangerous, but if they could perceive distance obviously the nearer object, although appearing identical in size to the other, would elicit more defensive reactions than the larger object. The results showed that this it did, indeed the larger more distant object caused no response at all. These defensive reactions in infants under two weeks were interesting from another point of view and that was that the infants had in fact only *seen* the object approaching, they had felt nothing. When a blast of air replaced the visual image there was no response. Therefore these young babies appeared to expect objects to be hard enough to hurt, otherwise there would have been no need for defence. Bower comments:

> In our culture, it is unlikely that an infant less than two weeks old could have been exposed to situations where he learnt to fear an approaching object and expect it to have tactile qualities. The only conclusion is that there is a primitive unity of the senses, with visual variables specifying tactile consequences: further, this primitive unity is built into the structure of the human nervous system. (1974:112–13)

A further experiment was then tried with newborn infants. When the infants wore polarizing goggles it was possible to produce a situation in which the infant saw an object that was not there so that when he reached for it there was nothing there to be felt (Bower, 1974:95). These newborn infants, when held, would grasp objects (or grasp the air when there was no object in view) but when they were wearing the goggles they would produce 'a howl' if the object they thought they saw turned out not to be there at all. Behaviour of this kind in such young babies certainly suggests that perceptually vision is dominant and that newborn babies are considerably more able than traditionally supposed.

However, some perceptual abilities do take time to develop. In an earlier experiment Bower (1966) showed that infants

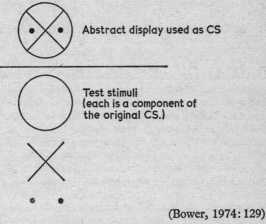

(Bower, 1974:129)

Fig. 3.8 *Visual stimuli*

initially responded to isolated elements of an object rather than to the object as a whole and that the integration of these elements was only achieved with age. When conditioned to respond to an abstract display small infants would respond to any of its components when they were presented in isolation and not until sixteen weeks did they respond only when the whole display was present (fig. 3.8).

It appears that infants use their perceptual information to construct a cognitive world (McGurk, 1974). We have seen that perceptually they are able to make complex and subtle discriminations at a very early age — how they use this ability to develop concepts, their cognitive building blocks, and how concepts are developed are the topics of the next chapter.

4
Conceptual development

Introduction

Over time the perceptually dominated world of the infant becomes the conceptual world of the adult. That is, the ability to order perceptual stimuli is developed. One way of ordering is to categorize such stimuli into various classes or sets. In order to understand that Class A is distinct from Class B the 'concept' of class A must have been formed; for example, a child may initially distinguish the class of animals from the class of objects, later make finer distinctions between types of animals, and finally be able to pick out breeds of dog as sub-classes of the class 'dog'. To develop the concept of 'animal' requires the child to know the ways in which animals are alike and, as a class, different from objects: that is he must know the distinguishing characteristics of animals. Concept development is therefore a development of both a classificatory system and the ability to apply such a system to the environment. It is an essentially human activity since there are no classes in nature – man classifies to suit his own purposes, although it is true that such classes will be based on observable differences and similarities which are present in nature. To this extent a class represents man's observation of natural attributes.

Concepts can be concrete or abstract: concrete ones like 'animals', 'objects', or 'blue objects', have concrete examples, whereas abstract concepts such as 'democracy', 'beauty', or 'truth' can only be used to describe objects or activities which, although very different from one another, have certain common aspects, namely the aspects designated by the abstract conceptual term.

A certain group of concepts, for example number, time, space

68

and causality, are of particular interest to Piaget, not because he is a psychologist but because he is an epistemologist, that is he is concerned with the nature of knowledge. The concepts studied by him are peculiar since it is not clear whether, for example, the concept of time is developed through experience or whether it must be present before events can be experienced temporally. In other words do we develop a concept of number, time, or space through living in a world which is quantifiable, changes over time, and is in space, or do we first have to have these concepts before we can begin to order the world in these terms? Piaget's studies suggest that such concepts are developed over time through the interaction of the organism and the environment, but the issue is not entirely resolved. However, since Piaget's epistemological concerns determine the types of concepts he has studied and since a great deal of work on concept development has been stimulated by Piagetian studies the emphasis has been on these particular concepts rather than on the more abstract concepts or on social concepts. There is therefore a certain imbalance in concept development studies and it should not be thought that the concepts most intensively studied are the only ones.

The process of concept development

How are concepts developed? This is an awkward question to answer since the process is internal and the experimenter has to externalize it without change or distortion through the experimental procedure. Studies of concept development are loosely of two kinds. Firstly, those which describe the stages a child passes through whilst he is in the process of acquiring a concept, and secondly, more detailed studies of the strategies a person employs.

Vygotsky (1962) found qualitative changes in concept development between childhood and maturity. His method was to present his subjects with twenty-two wooden blocks, which varied with respect to colour, shape, height and size. They were of six colours, six shapes, two heights—tall and squat, and two sizes of horizontal surface, large and small. On the reverse side of each block, and therefore hidden from the subject, was one of four nonsense words 'lag', 'bik', 'mur', and 'cev'. Irrespective of colour or shape 'lag' was written on the tall, large figures, 'bik' on the squat large ones, 'mur' on the tall, small ones, and 'cev' on the squat small ones. Firstly, the experimenter turned over one block and showed the subject its name. The subject had then to choose the other blocks that he thought might be examples of the concept. When he had tried to do this the experimenter would turn up a block chosen by the subject which was incorrect and show him its name. The experiment would continue in this way until the subject has either divided the blocks correctly or given up. The subject's cognitive processes were inferred from his method of dividing and sub-dividing the blocks.

Vygotsky argued that 'the ascent to concept formation is made in three basic phases. Each divided in turn into several stages'. (1962:59). Initially the children made unorganized heaps of things which chanced to be linked in their minds, these were highly unstable and there was no overall principle governing the admission or exclusion of new members to the set. The second phase showed a higher level of thinking in that by now the children thought in 'complexes', that is the objects were put together not just on the basis of connections which fleetingly existed in their minds but in terms of observable similarities between the objects. These links were, according to Vygotsky, 'concrete and factual' rather than 'abstract and logical'; that is, no one defining characteristic was abstracted. Rather, anything that had a connection with anything else was included. Five types of complexes were identified: first 'associative complexes', whereby a single common attribute was sufficient to put one block with another be it size, shape, colour, or location. Secondly, 'collections', when the principle appeared to be to collect a group which differed on one dimension, so that a child would collect all the different colours or all the different shapes. Thirdly, the 'chaining complex' appeared; an attribute of one block was used as the criterion for choosing the next block, when a different attribute would be chosen and this would then be matched with the next (so that a blue flat block led to a blue tall block followed by a tall red block, etc.) 'Diffuse complexes', were formed, which were similar to chains but the criteria were more vague, thus Vygotsky quotes triangles as being followed by trapezoids, trapezoids by squares, squares by hexagons, hexagons by semi-circles and semi-circles by circles. Finally, in this second phase there appeared 'pseudo complexes' in which the child would, for example, put all the triangles together and say they were 'murs'. This may look like a complex but when one block was turned over and 'cev' was revealed the child would remove that one block but keep the others together saying it was because 'they are triangles', not realizing that a single negative instance had invalidated his grouping system. It was not until around puberty that Vygotsky found the emergence of true conceptual thought and, even then, the child, having identified a concept, had great difficulty in defining it or explaining the basis for his formulation.

70

Vygotsky had made some progress towards identifying the stages in concept formation through the 'experimental' method and his approach is complemented by Piaget's 'clinical interview' in which the child is asked to perform a task and then questioned on his reasons for behaving in that particular way. Piaget calls a child's early concepts 'pre-concepts', since they are dominated by the immediate concrete situation and have no abstract or formal elements. He too found that a salient characteristic of such 'pre-concepts' was that the child juxtaposed elements which were alike rather than abstracting a unifying element which would act as a principle for inclusion or exclusion. Thus perceptual or functional similarity was considered sufficient basis for a grouping. It was only when schemes were developed and co-ordinated into structures that true concepts appeared. As we have seen (p. 16) Piaget believes that development takes place through conflict. In other words a child finds that the cognitive scheme he is using is inadequate and therefore has to make changes to take account of the new situation. Thus when a new concept is developed many behaviours, which are affected by this concept, will change. S–R theory, on the other hand, allows for discrete changes so that one behaviour can change but this will not affect other behaviour-patterns. Bower (1974) points out that these two theories lead to different predictions: if an infant has learnt one tracking task he could according to Piagetian theory transfer his learning to other tasks, whereas according to S–R theory he could not. When Bower compared groups of infants that had been exposed to conflict situations with groups which had not, he found that the experience of conflict did indeed accelerate development and learning *was* transferred.

In the fifties and sixties Bruner and his co-workers (Bruner 1956; 1966) performed a masterly series of experiments which gave much greater information concerning the actual process of concept attainment. Subjects were required to 'find the concept' embodied in a series of cards which were made up of figures and borders. The figures were either squares, circles, or crosses; they were coloured red, green, or black; and each card contained one, two, or three figures; the borders varied in number, either one, two or three (fig. 4.1). Concepts could therefore be of various kinds, for example, 'cards with red figures' or 'cards with one figure', 'cards with the same number of figures and borders', or 'cards with crosses', etc. The subjects were shown one card but not told what concept the experimenters had in mind. Their task was to discover the concept by asking whether other cards in the series were also exemplars.

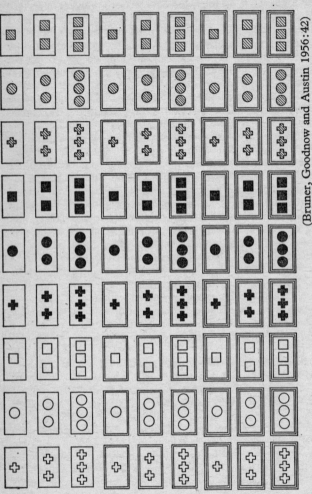

(Bruner, Goodnow and Austin 1956:42)

Fig. 4.1 An array of instances comprising combinations of four attributes, each exhibiting three values. Plain figures are in green, striped figures in red, solid figures in black

Bruner was concerned not with how concepts were formed but with how people search for defining attributes. When a person was attempting to attain a concept he had to make a series of decisions and his ways of dealing with the data were called by Bruner, Goodnow, and Austin (1956) 'strategies'. Four major strategies were identified: firstly, 'simultaneous scanning', which was exacting and required too great a load of memory and inference to be practicable (it meant the subject would have to evaluate all the possible hypotheses whenever he had a new piece of information). Secondly, 'successive scanning', when the subject tested one hypothesis at a time, such as 'is it the red one?', 'is it the circles?', etc. Thirdly, 'conservative focusing' in which the subject chose one card and worked through each of its attributes in turn so that when one attribute was shown to be negative he eliminated it; for example, if he chose as the focus card one that had three red circles with two borders the sequence would be:

1 Three red circles, two borders (+)-focus card.
2 Two red circles, two borders (+)-first choice: eliminate 'three figures' as a relevant attribute value.
3 Three green circles, two borders(−)-second choice: retain 'red' as a relevant attribute value.
4 Three red crosses, two borders (−)-third choice: retain 'circle' as a relevant attribute value.
5 Three red circles, one border (+)-fourth choice − eliminate 'two borders' as a relevant attribute value.
Ergo: concept in red circles (Bruner, Goodnow and Austin, 1956: 87).

The final strategy identified was 'focus gambling': here the subject took a focus card and varied more than one attribute at a time. This was potentially quicker and more economical than 'conservative focusing' but it was possible for it to take longer and therefore was only worthwhile if the reward for a quick solution was considerably greater than the loss for a slow one.

Ten years later Olson (1966) used these findings as a basis for an experiment to determine the strategies used by children aged three, five, seven and nine. The experiment had several variations but in essence ran as follows: children were shown a bulb board (fig. 4.2), some of whose bulbs would light up if pressed. These bulbs formed a pattern, which − until they were pressed − was 'hidden'. The children were given two cards printed with patterns, of which one corresponded to the pattern 'hidden' in the bulb board. By pressing bulbs, they had to discover which it was.

The experimenters were concerned with the way the child went about the task rather than whether they achieved a correct solution. Three problems were presented. There were two conditions: a free one to see 'what children would do' when allowed to press as many bulbs as they wished, and 'a constrained condition' to see what 'they could do when pressed' (1966:140). In this condition they only pressed one bulb at a time and were then asked if they knew which display was correct: if they did not they

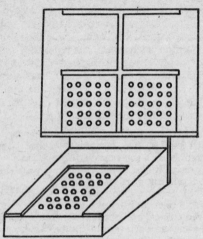

(Bruner, Olver, and Greenfield, 1966:138)

Fig. 4.2 *Apparatus used*

were instructed to press another bulb. The results showed that the youngest children used a 'search strategy' which was really no more than an attempt to see which bulb would light up with no reference to matching the pattern. The five-year-olds used a 'successive pattern matching strategy' in which they tried the whole of each display in turn. At seven, especially in the constrained condition, the 'information selection strategy' appeared, where again they were concerned with matching bulbs but chose their bulbs in a way which would give more information. Olson says of these strategies, 'they are programmes for finding and using information in certain specified ways: by encounter, by the search for matching images, and by the analysis of information (in the information theory sense of that word)' (1966:147). That is, cognitive development requires the ability to map, to locate, and to utilize information.

If to have a concept implies being able to order the environment and if the development of a concept both takes time and is the result of certain identifiable processes then the development of a specific concept should be observable in an individual, if the techniques of observation are sufficiently sensitive. By constructing concepts the individual creates a world that is in some sense his own, brings his views into line with those of others, and begins to appreciate the particular attributes of the material world.

(a) The object concept

One of the earliest distinctions an infant must make is the distinction between 'me and not me', and then differentiate the various aspects of the 'not me'. One important aspect of this is the presence of objects. We have seen (p. 66) that at a very tender age infants' response to objects suggest that they expect them to have certain qualities but when do they begin to appreciate other qualities such as permanence, whereby they realize that if, for example, an object changes location it can still be the same object?

Piaget (1951; 1953; 1955) believes that the concept of an object gradually matures. Initially the object itself is not distinguished from the child's act of looking, so that if the object disappears the child will continue to look at the place where it disappeared but make no attempt to search for it. At the next stage the child will attempt to search for the object, but if a cloth, in full view of the child, is placed over the object he will stop searching at once. The child will subsequently search for an object behind, for example, a screen but if, having found it behind screen A, the experimenter then places it behind screen B, the child will once again look behind screen A, even though he saw the experimenter put it behind screen B. In the second year the child will search for the object in a particular place if he sees it put there, but if the experimenter closes his hand over the object and then puts it behind the screen the child will look in the experimenter's hand but not behind the screen. Finally, at about eighteen months, the child will search in all the places where the object could have been placed thereby showing that the object has been conceptualized as a thing apart from his perception of it, his actions towards it, or the total milieu of which it had been thought to form a part, and he understands that it can remain the same even when displaced.

Bower (1974) has taken Piaget's data as a starting point and looked more closely at both the behaviour and the explanation given for it. If an infant ceases to search when an object is hidden under a cloth does it mean that the infant thinks the object is no longer there? Bower's investigations of these problems read like a first-class detective story of the Conan Doyle variety. Firstly, if the infant thinks an object disappears when hidden, he should be surprised if the object reappears when the cloth is removed: but, on the contrary, Bower found much greater surprise when the object did not reappear. This would suggest that the infant 'expected' it to be behind the screen. He then showed an infant a moving object which went behind the screen and then reappeared on the other side, the infant tracked it with his eyes so that he was looking at the other end of the screen at the right moment for the object to reappear, once again suggesting 'expectation'. But if Bower stopped the object just before it went behind the screen the child still tracked the now non-existent object, and appeared to expect it to reappear at the other end, even though it was, in fact, still in full view although stationary; it would therefore appear that the 'object that stops' is not identified with 'the object that moves'. This behaviour was even more in evidence when infants between twelve and sixteen weeks were shown an object that was stationary at point A move to point B, was stationary at point B, and then moved back to point A. These infants tracked it from A to B and B to A as many times as it shuttled back and forth, but if, after it stopped at B, instead of moving back to A it moved further along to another point, C, the infants would ignore the clearly visible object at C, and look towards A, showing obvious concern that it was not there. The infants appeared to be seeing several objects: namely, a stationary object at point A which disappeared and was replaced by a moving object, which disappeared and was replaced by the stationary object at point B; therefore, when the stationary object at point B disappeared, the infants expected it to reappear at A and were only confused by the appearance of yet another stationary object at point C. The development of the concept of object permanence did not seem to mature until about five months of age at which stage infants would begin to realize that the object could move but maintain its identity. They also, at this time, discovered that two objects could not be in the same place at one and the same time and that an identical object could not be in different places at one and the same time.

It is perhaps this knowledge that caused the infants problems when an object was hidden under a cloth. On the surface it may seem that if an infant can 'imagine' an object behind the screen and therefore expect it to reappear, he ought to be able to 'imagine' it under a cloth. However, if the infant thinks that two objects cannot be in the same place at the same time and if the cloth, or in

Bower's experiment a cup, is now in the place where the object had been then the infant thinks that the previous object must be somewhere else since its 'space' is taken up by the new object, that is the cloth or cup or whatever is covering it. That one object can be behind another appears to be understood, but the idea that one object can be inside another is beyond the infant's comprehension. Bower tested infants by showing them an object and immediately turning out the lights so that the room was in darkness. In the sense that the infants could not see anything, the object was out of sight. The infants' behaviour in the dark was recorded by using an infra-red-sensitive videcon camera and this showed that the infants did reach out and grasp the object which they could no longer see. When these same infants were tested in the conventional way, by seeing a cup being put over the object, they again stopped searching, Bower concludes that 'it is not true to say that "out of sight is out of mind" rather, the nature of the transition from "in sight" to "out of sight" is what determines or prevents successful hand and arm search'. (1974:207)

(b) The concept of number

In time infants develop the notion of 'inside' and, finally, towards the end of the sensori-motor stage the object concept becomes part of their cognitive structure. Once the child has realized that there are many instances of any object or event, he has to learn the properties of these objects or events and ways of ordering them – an important concept therefore is the concept of number. What exactly is involved in the concept of number?

There is a regrettable tendency for people to deplore illiteracy yet boast of being innumerate. However, a dislike of calculating or a suspicion of statistics does not mean that a person has no concept of number rather it reflects the refusal to use this concept in situations where it would be appropriate to do so. The concept of number involves the ability to classify and seriate and to unite these operations to express relations. For example, the number 4 expresses a class which is composed of four units, whether a unit is a bead or a nation. It also expresses that class as greater than the class of three units but less than the class of five units; that is, the child must understand both the relations between objects in a class and the relative position of this class to others. For a class of four units the cardinal number 4 describes the class but in order to arrive at this number the objects have to be counted in turn, or serially, and to that extent they differ; 'ordination', that is relating them to each other as first, second, third or fourth is necessary for the development of the concept, therefore 'cardination' refers to class and 'ordination' to relations and these two operations must fuse before the concept of number can be formed.

Piaget is particularly insistent that the child must be able to classify and seriate and must understand cardination and ordination before he can be said to have a concept of number. Cardination and ordination can easily become confused in a child's mind: take, for example, the situation in which the child is given ten dolls of graded height and ten toy walking sticks, also of graded heights, and is then asked to give each doll its stick. Here the smaller stick should be matched with the smallest doll and so on. Even getting the dolls in their correct order was too difficult for the youngest children, but once they could do this they could match the sticks to the dolls. A certain significant error did occur which was that if they were trying to match the fifth stick to the fifth doll they would use the fourth stick. It appeared that the child was confusing the original designation of the stick as 'the fifth' with the cardinal number of sticks that went before it, that is four.

Piaget conducted a series of experiments to test the child's understanding of addition and multiplication but he was not concerned with whether the child could, in an executive sense, perform the arithmetic manipulations but with whether he knew what he was doing. That the number concept is something that develops is shown by the fact that a child can deal with smaller sets of numbers, say those between one and fifteen, before he can deal with larger numbers and by the fact that a child begins by making empirical tests to help him to solve a problem rather than showing awareness of the necessary connections between the whole and its part. For example, when children below eight or nine were shown two sets of eight counters and agreed that there were the same number in each set and when one set was then divided into sub-sets of, say: two, three, and three: and the children were asked, in effect, if the sum total of the sub-sets, that is eight, was the same as the number of the original, undivided, set they would count the counters in the sub-sets before they answered.

Gréco (1962) noticed that when the child was shown two rows of counters with seven counters in each that were laid out so that one row was longer than the other he would say that each row had seven counters but that there were more in the longer row. Gréco observed that there appeared to be a lack of integration between the absolute and relative properties of the rows; that is each had the same number but in comparison one appeared to have more. The child seemed to conserve the number name, 'seven' (called by Piaget and Gréco *quotité*), before he learnt to conserve the quantity (*'quantité'*). This absolute relative distinction was taken up by Bryant (1974) when he argued that young children distinguished numbers relatively rather than absolutely; in addition to comparing *A* with *B* they also used the external framework in which *A* and *B* were presented and could therefore make statements about the relationships between *A* and *B* by means of their separate relationships to their common framework. This use of the external framework is particularly obvious when studying the perception of young children but it is also, Bryant maintains, a feature of their approach to number. He tested this by a discrimination experiment with four-year-olds. In this experiment children in two groups had to learn which of two pairs of cards they should choose. In the 'absolute' group they were shown two pairs of cards. In one pair one card had ten figures on it and the other twelve; in the second pair one card had twelve figures and the other fourteen. The children's task was to learn always to choose the card with twelve figures; another absolute group had a 20/22 and a 22/24 set of pairs. The 'relative' group were given the same pairs of cards but had to respond, not to the absolute number of twelve or twenty-two, but to the card which had most figures on it, the one with the relatively larger number, so that the card with twelve figures was correct in the 10/12 pair but incorrect in the 12/14 pair when, of course, the card with fourteen figures was the correct choice. The children found the relative task much easier and most of the four-year-olds failed to master the absolute discrimination. A relative code is obviously an inefficient way of dealing with number and a genuine concept of number requires an absolute code. Young children of three or four do appear to have an absolute sense of number below the number three but the ability at least to count and appreciate the logical connections between numbers is necessary before an absolute code can replace the relative one.

Hyde made a cross-cultural study in Aden of number and quantity. The questions she asked were: (1) Do Arab, Indian, Somali and European children living in Aden, faced with the same type of problem as Genevan children, exhibit characteristic responses analysable in terms of Piaget's 'stages'? (2) Are the 'stages' applicable to each test independently or do the tests represent a definite progression in the child's conception of number? (3) Is there any significant difference in the results obtained from children of different communities in Aden with respect to: (a) characteristic responses; (b) average age at which these appear? How do they compare with Piaget's norms? (1970:72). She tested first conservation of quantities (water and beaker test) and invariance of wholes (plasticine test). Secondly, she tested Cardinal and Ordinal one to one correspondence which involved the ability to seriate and to match the members of one series with the members of another. A neat test was the 'house and door test' in which the child was given ten wooden blocks of different sizes to represent the houses and ten pieces of plywood to represent the doors. The child was then told 'these are the houses and these are the front doors; arrange the houses and doors so that we can easily find the door that belongs to each house'. (1970:144) The final set of tests was to do with additive and multiplicative compositions, for example, the child would be given two piles of shells arranged so that there were eight shells in one pile and fourteen in the other and told to 'make this pile of shells and that pile of shells the same number' (1970:177). The children's replies were graded as C if complete misunderstanding of the task was evident; B if the child appeared to be at the stage described by Piaget as 'intuitive', that is if the child could not explain a correct performance, was misled by perceptual cues in some cases, or if he could solve a straightforward presentation of the problem but not when it was reversed; A if an entirely adequate answer was made.

The results showed that the behaviour of the children and their responses were almost identical to those given by the Genevan children except that the reasoning that appeared in type B answers was not always the same as that recorded by Piaget. The children, however, did not show a consistent progression in their level of success on the different tests, since children could be graded C on one test and A on another; two particularly unstable tests were the conservation tests (which were difficult for some and relatively easy for others) and the shells test (which was very easy for all the children except the Indians). There were, however, highly significant differences between the scores of the children of the same age in different communities (Table 4.A). Cross-cultural studies are often difficult to interpret since, as Goodnow (1969) points out, children of different nationalities may construe tasks differently and even if the children's answers are the same their method of reaching them may be different. Nevertheless to find a limited confirmation of Piaget's studies does suggest that the development of the number concept may have certain universal characteristics although the age at which a stage is reached may be a function of the environment. For example, a study of Mexican children (Price-Williams, Gordon, and Ramirez, 1969) showed that when a group of town children were matched with a group of country children with half of each group being the sons of potters, the potters' children were significantly more advanced in conservation

Table 4.A Analysis of variance – Piaget test scores
Each entry in the table below is the sum of the individual scores for that group. Each individual score consists of the total number of A's obtained by that individual over the 21 Piaget tests.

n = number in group
u = mean

		6 years	7 years	8 years
European	Boys	$u = 7\cdot67$ $n = 8$	$u = 9\cdot50$ $n = 8$	$u = 11\cdot25$ $n = 8$
	Girls	$u = 8\cdot01$ $n = 8$	$u = 11\cdot00$ $n = 8$	$u = 11\cdot50$ $n = 8$
Arab	Boys	$u = 3\cdot50$ $n = 8$	$u = 5\cdot25$ $n = 8$	$u = 6\cdot67$ $n = 8$
	Girls	$u = 3\cdot62$ $n = 8$	$u = 3\cdot62$ $n = 8$	$u = 5\cdot87$ $n = 8$
Indian	Boys	$u = 1\cdot25$ $n = 4$	$u = 3\cdot50$ $n = 4$	$u = 2\cdot50$ $n = 4$
	Girls	$u = 1\cdot5$ $n = 4$	$u = 4\cdot25$ $n = 4$	$u = 7\cdot75$ $n = 4$
Somali	Boys	$u = 0\cdot25$ $n = 4$	$u = 4\cdot50$ $n = 4$	$u = 5\cdot75$ $n = 4$
	Girls	$u = 1\cdot50$ $n = 4$	$u = 3\cdot75$ $n = 4$	$u = 8\cdot25$ $n = 4$

(Hyde, 1970:214)

of substance than the others and the trend was for them to show more understanding of conservation in general; presumably this advanced development could be attributed to the potters' children having more opportunities to play with clay and hence observing its attributes than their urban or rural peers.

In addition to his studies of the development of the concept of number, Piaget is noted for his investigation into children's understanding of weight, substance, movement, and space. But two other concepts are perhaps of more interest because they are fundamental and yet appear so abstract: these are the concepts of time and physical causality.

(c) *The concept of time*

To be able to tell the time does not mean that the child has a concept of time, since it may involve little more than learning how to read the figures on a dial without understanding what it is that they represent – beyond associating certain hours with certain events. Just as Piaget thinks classification and seriation to be integral to the concept of number so he (1946 a and b) links together time, movement, and velocity, although not so closely. It would appear that initially children believe that if two moving objects A and B, start at the same time and finish at the same time but A moves faster so that its finishing point is further away from the starting point than B's then A has both stopped later and taken longer. That is the children cannot co-ordinate time, distance travelled, and speed of travel or velocity. By the age of six to seven they will agree that the objects started and stopped at the same time but still maintain that A took longer.

Children's difficulties with time are reflected in their difficulties with age. Young children believe that size indicates age so that if one tree is bigger than another it must be older even though the trees may be of different types. Similarly if one child is born after another but grows taller, then the taller is thought to have become the older. The fact that children do not appreciate the continuous nature of time is illustrated by their claiming that they age a year on their birthday, so that overnight they become a year older.

(d) *The concept of causality*

One phenomenon that all children are exposed to is the phenomenon of change and a question of considerable interest is how children explain change to themselves. Piaget investigated children's views of causality by asking them questions both about natural phenomena, for example, why clouds move, why the sun and moon stay in the sky or the cause of shadows, and also about mechanical objects such as bicycles, steam-engines, trains, motor cars, and aeroplanes. The way the children's thinking develops can be illustrated by selecting certain answers given when Piaget asked children 'what makes a shadow'?:

Stage 1

Piaget   You know what a shadow is?
Stei (age 5) Yes, it's the trees that make them, under the tree.
Piaget   Why is there a shadow under the tree?
S   Because there are a lot of leaves, the leaves make it.
P   How do they they do it?
S   Because they are pink.
P   What does that do?
S   It makes a shadow.

P	Why?
S	Because inside (the leaves) it is night inside.
P	Why?
S	Because it's day on the top. The leaves are big and it is night inside them. (1930:184)

Stage 2

Piaget	Where does this shadow come from?
Leo (age 7)	From us.
P	How is it made?
L	It is made when he walks.
P	When it is night, does he make one too?
L	He makes one, then (but) you don't see it because it is night.
P	How do we make one?
L	You make it when you walk, because every step you make, it follows behind us.
P	Why does it follow us?
L	Because it is a person who makes it on the ground. (1930:186–7)

At the third stage Piaget found that Bab (aged eight years eleven months) could sometimes predict correctly but at other times thought that an object would throw a shadow during the night and on both sides:

Bab	It always make them but on the other side it makes them too.
Piaget	Why does it make a shadow in the night?
B	Because it has to.
P	Would you see it?
B	Oh no, because it is quite dark you couldn't see it. (1930:188–9)

At the fourth stage Piaget shows how Veil (aged nine and a half) will still give equivocal responses but further questioning shows that the concept has developed.

P	There is a house. The shadow is here. Where is the sun?
V	Here (correct prediction).
P	Why?
V	The sun comes from here. The house hides. It is dark behind: the sun can't go any further.
P	Why?
V	Because the house is large it hides the sun.
	(When shown an object which has been put in the shade Veil says:)
V	It doesn't make a shadow because it is already in the shadow.

83

P	It makes no shadow, or it does make it and we don't see it?
V	It doesn't make any. (1930:190)

Piaget (1930) distinguishes seventeen different types of causal relations in child thought and since they are so crucial to understanding the child's world and his cognitive development they are worth considering in detail. (1) The first is the 'motivational cause' whereby whatever happens is caused by God or man for a reason: God sends us dreams because we have done something wrong. (2) This is similar to the first but lacks the imputation of motive and consciousness, for example, the river is said to flow in order to go into the lake but this notion is taken no further hence Piaget's calling it 'finalism'. (3) 'Phenomenalistic causality' appears. Here anything is taken as a cause for anything else provided that some connection occurs to the child: the moon stays in the sky because it is yellow, or a pebble sinks because it is white. (4) This fourth form, 'participation', is frequent before the age of five to six and the child thinks that if two things are alike in some way one can cause the other so that shadows in a room are caused by the shadows outside. (5) A confusion between self and the world leads the child to believe in 'magical causality' whereby his wishes and gestures can affect the world. (6) The sixth, 'moral causality', may sound like the primitive 'motivational cause' but here the motive is a moral one, boats 'have to' float or they would be no use and drown their occupants.

This marks the end of stage one, stage two begins with (7) 'artificialist causality' which appears at the same time as 'moral' but differs from it in that human creativity is given as the explanation for the natural event. (8) 'Animistic causality' is the complement of 'artificialistic'. In this objects are thought to have internal 'motors' which enable them to carry out the commands they are given, thus the sun is what it is since it went on growing after it had been created by men. (9) Once animism is rejected objects are still thought of as having internal forces that explain their behaviour hence the name 'dynamic causality' for this form.

The third stage begins with the first truly physical explanation. (10) 'Reaction of the surrounding medium'. Now motives and intentions are no longer evoked, the child is genuinely seeking to answer the questions 'how?' Clouds still set themselves moving but, having started, they are driven along by the air caused by their movement. (11) 'Mechanical causality' appears between the ages of seven and eight after the elimination of dynamism when children will say that the wind pushes the clouds or the pedals are responsible for the movement of a bicycle. (12) 'Causality by generation' responses are given in reply to questions concerning how things began and the child will say that the sun came out of a fiery cloud and clouds come out of smoke. (13) Between the ages of eight and ten the notion that all things have grown is replaced by the idea that they may be the result of a fusion of discrete elements so that the sun is described as being formed by a group of clouds that 'roll themselves up into a ball'. (14) Children now develop 'schemes of condensation' whereby explanations are related to the density of things, for example, stones are hard because the earth is close packed, water is light because it is liquid. (15) 'Atomistic composition' leads children to say that stones are made of little stones or grains of sand. (16) 'Spatial explanation' can appear after the age of nine or ten but Piaget says it is a rare form since it involves the child in explaining for instance the rise in water-level, when an object is immersed, in terms of the volume of the immersed object. (17) The final form of explanation is 'explanation by logical deduction' and it increases from ages ten to eleven. The child uses developed concepts such as density and weight and the concepts chosen are not imposed by the apparent facts but by the types of logical deduction which are necessary.

If the child's causal concepts are those Piaget describes, their difficulties with other concepts become more understandable. If inanimate objects are, initially, thought to have motives, or to respond to man's wishes, then it is hardly surprising that children do not see the necessity for thinking in terms of the conservation of substance or the invariance of numbers, since the material world is not conceived of in this way. The integrated nature of concept development leads the child from a floating magical view of the world to one that is both more orderly and, apparently, more realistic: when conceptual thought is fully established Alice is no longer in Wonderland.

5
Theories of language acquisition

Introduction

Students attempting to make sense of the study of language acquisition may be forgiven for seeing it as 'an undertaking of great advantage but nobody to know what it is' (Company Prospectus of the South Sea Bubble quoted in Adams, 1972:267). There are two main reasons for the confusions and frustrations; first, the emphasis placed by educationalists on 'language' as a determinant of school achievement, and second, a confusion between 'psycholinguistics' and 'sociolinguistics'. The first of these leads people to hope that the study of language acquisition will solve the problems of language deficit. But language acquisition is only marginally concerned with this, since, as studied by psychologists, it is an attempt to understand the development of linguistic competence and performance, that is both the actual spoken language (performance) and the underlying knowledge of linguistic, semantic, and syntactic categories such as agent and object or nouns and verbs, which make such spoken language possible (competence). These aspects are developed by *all* children and individual differences, especially with respect to competence, are not significant. Secondly, to confuse 'psycholinguistics' with 'sociolinguistics' leads people to expect answers to types of problems not, in fact, raised by the questions asked. 'Psycholinguistics' is to do with individual language and behaviour; 'sociolinguistics' is the study of the social role of language. Thus the psychologist is primarily interested in 'linguistic competence' – that is the person's underlying knowledge of his language which must be present before he can produce speech; whereas the socio-

Paragraph 2, 3, 4, deal with relationship between language and thought.

logist studies 'communicative competence' which is concerned with the appropriate use of speech in different social settings. Children who appear to be less articulate than others are unlikely to suffer from a lack of linguistic competence. Their word order is not jumbled nor do they use nouns where others would use verbs, but from a lack of communicative competence, so that for them speech is an unsatisfactory vehicle for communication. All human beings, as far as we know, share a common linguistic competence, but different social groups are more or less competent as communicators. This would imply that if there is a correlation between language use and school achievement the origins of deficit are social rather than psychological, although it is often difficult in practice to untangle the two aspects.

In the last decade language acquisition has been studied more intensively than ever before. The topic has always been attractive to psychologists concerned with child development, who intuitively believed that language was a significant factor in human development and was related both to thought and to cognition. Lately new developments in linguistics have made a more intensive study of early language possible in that, as linguists have developed more precise formal methods for describing language so it has become possible for psychologists to use their formal frameworks as a way of ordering the mass of data generated by a child's spontaneous speech. Cooperation between linguists and psychologists has generated some fruitful hypotheses concerning both the nature of language and the child's world.

Already psychologists have had to think harder about the role they intuitively gave to language. First, was it important in an evolutionary sense? Roger Brown (1973) suggests that it is the social, communicative function of language which has been most important since by means of language man can transmit and receive information, even from those long dead, thus enabling individual man to transcend the limits of his own experience. He, however, does not believe that, in an evolutionary sense, man's linguistic powers are responsible for his cognitive powers: 'unfortunately we know next to nothing about what language has done for thought, and we cannot even be sure that language has importantly affected the power of thought'. (1973:38)

The relationship between language and thought has generated a great deal of speculation and research. In the sixties Vygotsky's position had great appeal. He argued that thought and speech had different roles but that their development, although separate, was not mutually exclusive – at times the two developmental processes came together but they always diverged again. Thus, he says, there is a 'pre-intellectual' stage in speech and a 'pre-linguistic' stage in thought, but thought and speech do come together and at this point thought becomes verbal and speech rational. From this he develops his theory of word meaning:

[margin note: Deals with Vygotsky]

> The meaning of a word represents such a close amalgam of thought and language that it is hard to tell whether it is a phenomenon of speech or a phenomenon of thought. A word without meaning is an empty sound; meaning, therefore, is a criterion of 'word', its indispensable component. It would seem, then, that it may be regarded as a phenomenon of speech. But from the point of view of psychology, the meaning of every word is a generalization or a concept. And since generalizations and concepts are undeniably acts of thought, we may regard meaning as a phenomenon of thinking. It does not follow, however, that meaning formally belongs to two different spheres of psychic life. Word meaning is a phenomenon of thought only in so far as thought is embodied in speech, and of speech only in so far as speech is connected with thought and illumined by it. It is a phenomenon of verbal thought, or meaningful speech – a union of word and thought. (1962: 120)

Piaget's theory is somewhat different (see p. 26) but Vygotsky is in agreement with Piaget that action precedes words: 'The word was not the beginning – action was there first; it is the end of development, crowning the deed!' (1962: 153)

Today neither view is thought to be entirely satisfactory, rather psychologists are inclined to agree that thought and language have separate roots but that language is particularly relevant for certain cognitive tasks. Hence they concentrate on the nature of these tasks.

To tease out the relationship between language and cognition requires considerable conceptual and experimental expertise. A problem raised by Vygotsky's view is that if language and thought have different roots, and if thought is related to sensori-motor practical intelligence to what is language related? A plausible hypothesis would be that language is also rooted in sensori-motor behaviour. Piaget himself (1949) remarked that the children's first, single word, utterances could be expressions of action patterns. Sinclair-de-Zwart (1973) adds weight to this hypothesis by pointing out that the first grammatical relations used by the child, subject-predicate and object-action, mirror the first cognitive distinctions the child makes between the self as agent and objects as external. It is thus possible that sensori-motor behaviour is the basis for both language and for operational thinking.

Herbert H. Clark (1973) argues that, with respect to space and time, language and cognition can be separated in that what the child does is to apply spatial and temporal terms in order to express the knowledge he has already gained concerning space and time through living on this planet. The relationship may, however, be closer in that it is likely that the first linguistic forms to appear are those which express the meanings the child has developed but he may also have developed meaningful notions which he cannot express linguistically. Confirmatory evidence of this is given by Slobin's (1973) consideration of two girls who were bilingual in Hungarian and Serbo-Croatian. Before the age of two when speaking Hungarian the children were expressing notions of direction and position e.g. 'into', 'out of', 'on top of' etc. but they did not express such notions in Serbo-Croatian. It happens that it is more complex, linguistically, to express direction and position in Serbo-Croatian than in Hungarian and therefore we can see that it is possible for a child to have developed cognitively but to be inhibited by linguistic complexity. In summary, the study of the acquisition of language is intimately related to cognitive development but can be studied separately. Even if such studies are not concerned with language deficit nor subsequent achievement they have an intrinsic interest.

How, then, do psychologists study language acquisition? There are two main ways: the first is to record and transcribe the spontaneous speech of one or more children over a period of time by paying visits to the child's home and recording all that the child says, and all that is said to him, during the visit. This was the method used in a famous series of studies, by Roger Brown and his associates at Harvard, of three children – Adam, Eve, and Sarah. Adam and Eve were recorded for two hours every two weeks and Sarah for one half hour every week. They studied Eve for one year and Adam and Sarah for five years and the data thus obtained was, and still is, being analysed. Obviously this is an immensely laborious method and most studies of this kind have a very small sample but they are intensive. The second method is experimental: here the experimenter concentrates on a specific aspect of child speech and sets up tasks to see how children perform on them. An example of this approach is the study by Donaldson and Balfour (1968) of children's use of 'more' and 'less'. For their experiment with three-year-old children they had two cardboard apple trees on which they could hang up to six apples. They would then vary the number of apples on each tree and ask the child questions such as, 'Does one have more/less apples on it than the other?' or ask the children to make the trees have the same number of apples, or more or less. What they found was that the children could not differentiate between 'more' and 'less', in most cases 'less' was used as if it meant 'more'.

Some definitions

(1) What exactly do we mean when we say that a child acquires language? Rather obviously, it means that a child learns to talk to his parents and to others but the real question is, what must the child have learnt in order to be able to talk? A language is a rule-governed series of signals related to events; in order to correctly generate such signals the speaker must have an implicit knowledge of grammar and the meanings coded by grammar. Likewise the hearer must have a similar knowledge in order to decode the signals. Thus to develop a language is not to develop one linguistic aspect but several and then to co-ordinate them appropriately. Firstly, a language is composed of sounds – it has a phonological system; these sounds when put together make words, which are joined into sentences – that is a language has a syntactic system which governs how one sign is related to another sign, and it has a 'meaning' or semantic system which regulates the relation between signs and their meanings. Thus a child must learn the phonological, syntactic, and semantic rules and this learning process is the process of language acquisition.

The first sound that an infant makes is a cry and spectrographic analysis of infant cries has shown that they vary from infant to infant and that they can reflect the infant's physiological state (Lind, Truby, and Bosma, 1965). The infant soon begins to emit a series of sounds – cries, gurgles, coos, and chuckles but these vocalizations are not words, they represent Vygotsky's 'pre-intellectual' stage in that they do not encapsulate a concept and, strictly speaking, they are not linguistic, but by the babbling stage they may have a social function and, if language is primarily communicative, then they can be said to have one linguistic feature – that of being social. This early babbling cannot be imitative as infants produce sounds that they are not hearing. For example, American children produce the French 'r' and congenitally deaf children babble for a time and then stop. The social nature of babbling was shown in an early study by Rhinegold (1959). This study started from the observation that infants vocalize as part of their response to the appearance of an adult. The question asked was whether the frequency of vocalization could be increased if the adult responded to it directly. The experiment was as follows: twenty-one normal infants aged three months and living in an institution were the experimental subjects;

eleven were studied in Experiment I with experimenter A; and ten different subjects plus one from Experiment I were studied in Experiment II by experimenter B. During the first two days, called the baseline days, the experimenter would lean over the subject's cot and the number of vocalizations was counted and recorded. During the next two days, the first and second conditioning days, the experimenter responded to, or reinforced, the infant subject's vocalizations by smiling, clucking, and touching his abdomen. During the last two days, the extinction days, the experimenter behaved as she has in the first two baseline days. The results indicated that, firstly, there was no difference between Experiment I and Experiment II, secondly vocalization increased on the conditioning days, and thirdly, extinction caused the vocalizations to decrease to around the original level. Therefore these infants did increase their babbling when it caused a response and decreased it when it ceased to do so. This experiment says nothing about babbling when the mother, or mother substitute, is absent but there are several theories: one is that the sound which the infant hears is itself reinforcing, another that it imitates its mother and is reinforced by hearing itself sound like its mother. After the babbling stage the infant's phonemic perception and production must increase in order for him to be able to abstract and apply the phonological rules of his native language, but the study of this is in its very early stages.

Once the child begins to combine words in order to express relations within a sentence, for example the relation of subject and predicate or affirmative and negative, he has to learn the syntax of his language. It is in the area of the acquisition of syntax that the most interesting advances were made in the sixties, and they need to be understood even if subsequent work has gone beyond them. The impulse for these new developments was the work of the M.I.T. linguist Naom Chomsky. He began by pointing out that every day we hear thousands of sentences which are unique, that is they are not exactly like any we have heard before, and yet we have no difficulty in understanding them. We easily recognize the difference between a random jumble and an orderly sequence of ideas even if the sequence does not make sense. Consider his example 'colourless green ideas sleep furiously' and 'furiously sleep green ideas colourless', both of these are unlikely to have been heard before and both are meaningless, yet we have no difficulty in recognizing the first as grammatical and the second as a muddle. Our capacity to distinguish the one from the other shows that we know implicitly what is meant by orderly English. This implicit knowledge, when formalized, constitutes the syntactic rules. Conventional grammatical parsing is a totally inadequate way of formalizing this knowledge.

Chomsky proposes a 'transformational grammar' which is based on a most important distinction between the 'surface' structure and the 'deep' structure of a sentence. If we take the two sentences, 'John is easy to please' and 'John is eager to please' we can see that they have the same surface structure and yet John is object of the first sentence and the subject of the second. Alternatively sentences may have a different surface structure but the same deep structure, for example 'John ate the orange' and 'the orange was eaten by John'. Thus the different surface structures can refer to the same deep structure, that is to a particular relationship between John and the orange. A transformational grammar attempts to produce a system of rules which will 'generate' sentences, to show that each sentence has a deep and surface structure, and to show the relations between the two. It is obvious that the surface structures of different languages are very different. On the other hand if there were no common ground between languages it would be impossible to translate one into another. It may be that at some level all languages share a common deep structure. The features which all languages share are called by Chomsky 'linguistic universals'. The differences between languages can therefore be thought of as distinct sets of rules for transforming the common deep structure into a variety of surface structures.

As well as making the distinction between deep and surface structure Chomsky also distinguishes a speaker's 'competence' from his 'performance'. Linguistic competence refers to the ability of a language user to apply the rules of his language in order to associate sounds and meanings. Performance is the actual observed use of language. Competence is therefore one step away from performance, it represents the knowledge a native speaker must have in order to understand any of the almost infinite number of sentences in his language. Performance is the expression of competence in speaking or listening to speech. A person may be competent to deal with an unlimited number of grammatical sentences but his performance may be impaired.

We can therefore distinguish between studying behaviour and studying the system of rules underlying it. The study of the acquisition of language can thus be thought of as the study of the development of competence. Following on from Chomsky's work on transformational grammar linguists began to concentrate on the semantic aspects of language, that is those parts which are to do with meaning, and the seventies have seen the development of 'case' grammar. The distinction between syntax and semantics can be illustrated by using syntax to refer to such relations as 'subject' and 'object', and semantics to refer to relations such as 'agent', 'patient' or 'instrument'. In other words 'syntax serves a semantic purpose – it is the organization of words within sentences for the expression of meanings' (Edwards, in press).

'Cases' are basically the 'roles' played by persons or things in the actions or states identified by a sentence. For example, if we say 'Paul opened the bottle in the hall', then in this sentence the units 'Paul', 'the bottle' and 'the hall' each have a particular 'role': 'Paul' is the 'agent', he was the one who *opened* the bottle; 'the bottle' is the patient, that is it is what was affected by Paul's action; and 'the hall' expresses the location where the opening took place. At present different linguists use different terms but Roger Brown's table, adapted from Chafe, is a clear introduction to 'roles' and their application (Table 5A, p. 94).

The linguist's original interest in transformational grammar to which is now added an interest in case grammar is paralleled by psychological studies originally of the acquisition of syntax and latterly the acquisition of ways of expressing semantic relations. Both methods of approach have been stimulating and we have considerably increased our understanding of child language over the last ten years but it cannot be denied that these studies are in their early stages and therefore at present conclusions should be seen as tentative. If the above distinctions between the phonological, syntactic, and semantic aspects of language are fairly clear we may now proceed to a brief survey of the various theories of language acquisition in a quasi-historical sequence. It is necessary to do this rather than concentrate on the most recent theory since each theory represents either a development of, or a reaction to, an earlier one and therefore cannot be understood in isolation.

Theories of language acquisition

(a) *Behaviourist*
One of the earliest theories was perhaps the most obvious, namely that the child learns language in response to adult stimuli. This theory is associated with the behaviourist B. F. Skinner who said that since speech is a motor response the learning model which would be the most appropriate is the 'operant' one – that is a random action is rewarded and because of the reward it is repeated, and again rewarded, until the originally random action becomes part of the person's behavioural repertoire. In the case of speech the reinforcement is always social and Skinner has several suggestions as to how a speech response may arise. Firstly, it may be

Table 5.A Some semantic roles played by noun phrases in simple sentences

Role	Definition	Examples
Agent	Someone or something which causes or instigates an action or process. Usually animate but not always, an agent must be perceived to have its own motivating force.	*Harriet* sang. *The men* laughed. *The wind* ripped the curtains.
Patient	Someone or something either in a given state or suffering a change of state.	*The wood* is dry. He cut *the wood*.
Experiencer	Someone having a given experience or mental disposition.	*Tom* saw the snake. *Tom* wanted a drink.
Beneficiary	Someone who profits from a state or process, including possession.	*Mary* has a convertible. This is *Mary's* car. Tom bought *Mary* a car.
Instrument	Something that plays a role in bringing about a process or action but which is not the instigator; it is used by an agent.	Tom opened the door with *a key*. Tom used *his knife* to open the box.
Location	The place or locus of a state, action, or process.	The spoon is in *the drawer*. Tom sat in *the chair*.
Complement	The verb names an action that brings something into existence. The complement, on a more or less specific level, completes the verb. This use of the word 'complement' is not, incidentally, its most common use in linguistics.	Mary sang a *song* John played *checkers*.

Source: Adapted from Chafe, 1970.   (Brown, 1973:8)

learned as an 'echoic' response, that is the child may imitate a sound it hears the parent making and the parent will reward the imitation if it is sufficiently like the original stimulus. Secondly, it may be learned as a 'mand', in this case the child utters a random sound which causes the parent to respond and if this response happens to fulfill a present need of the child then he will repeat the former randomly produced sound. For example, a parent might take a random utterance of the child as sounding like 'milk', the parent then gives the child some milk and if this is reinforcing the child will learn to use 'milk' appropriately. Thirdly, the verbal response may be acquired as a 'tact', that is, if a child makes a certain sound when faced with a particular stimulus and is rewarded for this he will repeat the sound whenever the stimulus appears. A learning theory of this kind stresses the non-linguistic situation in which the adult acts either as a stimulus or as a reinforcement. Words or groups of words are thought to be sorted into groups on the basis of the behaviour with which they are associated. For example the names of objects would be associated with manipulation by the child or demonstration by an adult. Words of praise or blame which are used to shape the child's behaviour would form another category.

(b) *Structural*
The above explanation was held by Chomsky (1959) and his associates to be totally inadequate. They argued that the infinite number of sentences that a child can recognize and can, in theory, produce from the finite number of sentences he actually hears cannot be explained in stimulus-response terms. McNeill characterizes earlier studies of language by saying that 'The basic assumption appears to have been that child language was adult language filtered through a great deal of cognitive noise and impoverished of vocabulary' (1966:16). A considerable amount of misunderstanding may have arisen in earlier studies by linguists noticing that child language was different from adult language and assuming therefore that it was a deficient form of adult language, whereas, as is so often the case in the history of science, a new formulation of the problem led to new insights. McNeill concentrated on the characteristics of the child's distinctive language saying that, 'Recent studies look upon a young child as a fluent speaker of an exotic language'. (1966:16) A second cause of confusion is that the Skinnerian theory may well account for the fact that an English child will say 'milk' and a French child 'lait' that is for differences in surface structure, but sentences are more than the sum total of the words of which they are composed. A des-

cription of a sentence requires a description of the relationships between the words and what the psychologist has to do is to trace the development of the child's knowledge of these relationships.

Let us start from the empirical observation that a child's original output consists of one word, and, later, two word utterances. The single word utterances are often called 'holophrastic' which means that they represent a wide range of meanings, that at this stage a child will use one word where an adult would use a sentence. Susan Ervin-Tripp gives two lists of early utterances (1973:265) and, as she points out, the interesting thing about these lists is that the first was drawn from Luo children in Kenya (Blount, 1969) and the second from Samoan children (Kernan, 1969), thus showing universal similarity between the speech of

Table 5.B Early utterances

List A	*List B*
Cigarette down	Girl rides
Give me candy	Bring candy
Candy mine	Baby's eyes
Hit you	Baby fall
Give me banana	Put down
You eat?	Baby walks
I want water	Wants sleep
Ball there	Keith
Go home	Go
This visitor	Your baby

(Tripp in Moore, 1973:265)

children at this stage. (Table 5B). These early utterances usually consist of words which in an adult analysis would be classed as nouns together with words which modify the nouns. Braine (1963) divided these words into two classes: 'pivot' and 'open'. The 'pivot' class consists of a small number of functional words such as 'all gone' 'big', 'more' and 'my', and the 'open' class of a large number of content words, for example 'boy', 'sock', 'plane' 'daddy'. Therefore the first rule in a child's competence could be 'a sentence is a pivot class word plus an open class word'. From the point of view of adult grammar the pivot class contains adjectives, verbs, and pronouns. Gradually the child distinguishes these types of modification and hence differentiates syntactic classes. At the same time these differentiations are appropriately integrated into sentences until the child's sentences syntactically approxi-

96

mate to those of adults. Brown comments 'The very intricate simultaneous differentiation and integration that constitute the evolution of the noun phrase is more reminiscent of the biological development of an embryo than it is of the acquisition of a conditioned reflex'. (1964:151)

The question, however, which interested psychologists was not what the child was doing but how he was able to do it. In the first place an infant is exposed to a great deal of noise – coughing, crying, phones ringing, and speech – how does he know to attend to the speech elements rather than the other noises in his environment? Secondly, how is it that children are able to acquire this complex system of language so rapidly? And, thirdly, how, out of the mass of speech that they hear, are they able to abstract sufficient to start speaking themselves? The answer proposed by Chomsky was that the child must have some *innate* idea of what to look for so that he pays attention to some types of utterance rather than others. Chomsky (1965) suggests that each child has a Language Acquisition Device (LAD) which enables him to attend to and abstract what is necessary from the speech he hears around him, process what he hears and thus produce his own grammatical competence. The internal structure of LAD is given by the linguistic universal, that is those linguistic features which are common to all languages. Chomsky argues that there is, for instance, a universal hierarchy of word categories so that at the top we would have the category 'all words', then 'nouns' and 'verbs', then 'types of noun' etc. If a child had an innate knowledge of this he would be able, by working down it, to develop all the categories of adult grammar. This assumes that the basic grammatical relations of 'subject' and 'object' etc. are also universal and support is given to this supposition by Greenberg's finding (1963) that in a survey of thirty languages there appeared to be no language lacking such concepts so that a child who had an innate knowledge of them could acquire any natural language merely by finding out how his particular language expressed these universal concepts common to all languages.

McNeill (1970 a and b) maintains that all children have an innate concept of a sentence which gives rise to their initial hypothesis that a sentence consists of single words. As the child is exposed to his native language he develops new particular hypotheses related to the nature of the particular language to which he happens to have been exposed. The reason why children of all linguistic communities have an initial stage of one and then two word utterances is that their innate endowment consists of the linguistic universals which, of course, are, by definition, common to all languages. Therefore when the child is first exposed to language he has the capacity to scan the linguistic data before him and recognize examples of distinctions which are the same as those in the universal system of categories. He can, therefore, both react to what is appropriate and organize it in such a way that his output is to some extent consonant with the speech that he is hearing, and since both adult and child share a competence which is based on the linguistic universals the adult is able to interpret the child's early attempts to work out the rules of the particular form of language to which he has been exposed, be it English, French, or Japanese.

This theory of Chomsky, McNeill, and others differs fundamentally from that of Skinner in that they see the child's unique early language as being initially limited to the base or deep structure of sentences, springing from an innate knowledge or awareness of the linguistic universals, and gradually developing transformations so that the child becomes capable of converting the base structure to surface structure. McNeill summarizes the essential difference by saying:

> If children begin their productive linguistic careers with a competence limited to the base structure of sentences, it is difficult to see how it can be explained by any theory of language acquisition that restricts attention to what a child might obtain from the observable surface characteristics of parental speech. Such theories would have to predict the opposite course of development: first, surface structure; then, base structure. Most behaviourist theories have assumed this order, with notable lack of success; failure is inevitable when children produce only the base structure, and behaviourist theories produce only the surface structure of sentences. What is needed is either a child who commences acquisition with surface structure or a theory that focuses on base structure. Since it is easier to change theories than children, the latter course has been followed here. (1966:52)

(c) Biological

Sometimes explanations seem to raise as many problems as they solve. The idea that certain aspects of linguistic competence are innate is an example of this. But in the mid and late sixties studies of child language were considerably enriched by the insights of Eric Lenneberg (1964 and 1967) whose interest was in the *biological* foundations of language. To say that something is biologically specific to our species may be to approach 'the innate' in a more constructive way. There are also interesting parallels between his approach and Piaget's, which is hardly surprising as both start from the very reasonable point that man is a particular type of biological organism.

Here we will consider three aspects of Lenneberg's theory: first, his belief that language is species specific; secondly the relationship between language and cognitive functioning; and, thirdly, whether the development of language is biologically determined. Lenneberg asks whether man has biological endowments that make the human form of communication uniquely possible for our species. He thinks so and gives five reasons. First, language capacity is related to the way that the various parts of the human brain work together, in other words to its particular mode of functioning. To illustrate this he takes the example of a nanocephalic dwarf who has a brain which is as small as that of an animal and yet who acquires language. It is not brain size which is important so much as the way in which that brain is organized. Secondly, the developmental schedule for language learning is the same for all humans even those who are mentally retarded. Children with very low I.Q.'s develop language in the same sequence as normal children, the only difference being that the retardates may not progress as far as normals. Thirdly, it is very difficult to suppress language learning – with even a minimal amount of stimulation children will begin to speak. Fourthly, he maintains that language cannot be taught to any other species. This may be more in doubt today but when Lenneberg wrote (in 1964) experiments in teaching language to chimpanzees had not produced any really significant results. Lastly, he refers to the existence of language universals saying that we are capable of learning any language and human languages have more in common with each other than they have with any form of nonhuman communication.

With reference to language and cognitive functioning there are certain cerebral functions which mediate between sensori input and motor output called by Lenneberg cognitive functioning, this is responsible for man's ability to categorize in specific ways, solve problems (see A7) and form learning sets (see A3). Developmentally the infant begins by organizing what he can see, hear, taste, touch or smell in his environment and organizing the motor movements of his muscles. General principles of differentiation and categorization are the basis for both types of organization and these general principles appear in specialized form in verbal behaviour. Thus words are not merely labels for objects. Rather they stand for a cognitive process, which Lenneberg defines operationally as 'the ability to make a similar response to different stimulus situations within given limits (1967:355–356) which

99

presupposes that the child is able to recognize similarities and differences in the environment and respond appropriately. Language, then, 'is the manifestation of species-specific cognitive properties. It is the consequence of the biological peculiarities that make a human type of cognition possible' (1967:374). If the above view is correct then the biological basis of human cognition will delimit the range of linguistic possibilities, but within these limits many variations are possible so that the outer form, the surface structure of language, may vary but the underlying, deep or base, structure will be invariant.

Developmentally this biological basis will determine the form of cognition and language and while it is true that an external stimulus may be necessary to stimulate the onset of speech, these external stimuli are not responsible for the way in which language develops. When an individual is maturationally ready to behave in a certain way he will not exhibit this behaviour in the absence of an 'environmental trigger' but this environmental impulse has only an initiatory function – it is not the cause of the behaviour. At a certain point in maturation the child's cognitive processes have reached a state of 'language readiness', which Lenneberg says stretches from about age two to fourteen, but initially the language structure is latent, development is the process of actualization by means of which this latent structure is transformed into realized structure.

Lenneberg's summary of the process of language acquisition is distinctive yet similar to Piaget's:

> If language is an aspect of a fundamental, biologically determined process, it is not scientifically profitable to look for a *cause* of language development in the growing child just as we do not look for a *cause* for the development of his ears. It might be more fruitful to think of maturation, including growth and the development of behaviour such as language, as the traversing of highly unstable states: this disequilibria, producing further rearrangements and so on until relative stability, known as *maturity*, is reached. Language-readiness is an example of such a state of disequilibrium during which the mind creates a place into which the building blocks of language may fit. (1967:376)

(d) *Theories of meaning*

The theories discussed so far have been primarily concerned with the development of syntax, with the structure of child language. But recently interest has shifted to the question of what the child *means* when he speaks, in other words to the question of his semantic intentions. The early pivot/open distinction can be seen to be inadequate once semantic intentions are involved, for example Brown (1973) found four distinct functions expressed by the seemingly simple pivot and open construction:

1 Pointing and naming ('that –').
2 Commenting on or requesting recurrence of a referent ('more –').
3 Commenting on or requesting the disappearance of a referent ('all-gone –').
4 Noticing or attracting the notice of a referent already present ('hi –').

Likewise Bloom (1970) pointed out that the pivot/open distinction did not elucidate ambiguous forms, for example, 'mummy sock' could mean 'mummy's sock' or 'mummy is putting my sock on'.

This approach to language acquisition by studying the child's semantic development makes the question of how and why the child learns meaning central and moves the investigation closer to a sociolinguistic approach since semantic sentential relations such as 'agent', 'patient', and 'instrument' can only develop when the child has been exposed to a social situation in which they are relevant. Halliday (in press) suggests that language acquisition should be seen as the development of the 'function' or 'use' of language in such a way that each of these functions has an associated 'meaning potential'. He hypothesizes that there are three phases of development. First, a period when the most basic functions of language are acquired, for example:

Instrumental – 'I want'.
Regulatory – 'do as I tell you'.
Interactional – 'me and you'.
Personal – 'here I come'.
Heuristic – 'tell me why'.
Imaginative – 'let's pretend'.
Informative – 'I've got something to tell you'.

In the second phase there are major advances: (1) the use of vocabulary. (2) The development of two new groups of functional structures – the one the 'Pragmatic' (which is to do with using language both to satisfy the child's own needs and as a means of controlling the actions of others or interacting with them), the other the 'Mathetic' (or learning function of language based on observation and comment – 'red car' or 'two books'). These two functions would come together if for example the child said 'some chocolate – give me some'. (3) The development of dialogue which requires an awareness of linguistic role – whether that of addresser or addressee. There is a considerable amount of development necessary before the child can engage in dialogue in the way that adults take for granted.

In the third phase the child approaches adult language in that each of his utterances is no longer representative of a single use of language but is beginning to mark the adult functional distinction between 'ideational' and the 'interpersonal'. By 'ideational' is meant a person's observations and interpretations of events and by 'interpersonal' his reactions to these events in terms of attitudes or wishes. Halliday characterizes the first as the 'observer' function of language and the second as the 'intruder' function.

There is thus a developmental sequence from phase 1 when function is equated with use; through the development, in phase two, of the Pragmatic and Mathetic functions and dialogue, to, in phase three, the observance of the adult 'ideational' and 'interpersonal' functions. This means that in learning language the child is also learning the constituents of the social world in which he finds himself through the interactive linguistic process whereby he is both able to assign and accept roles, and to observe and play a part in the world.

6
Specific aspects of language acquisition

Phonological development

The phonological system of a language consists of both the sound system and the 'prosodic' system, that is the system of intonation, of stress, and of pauses. In order to acquire phonological competence in his native language the child must first distinguish segmental variations which are smaller than words. These could be single sound differences, 'cat' versus 'rat', or differences expressing tense number or case; or again, they could be the differences between 'voiced' (Z and V) and 'unvoiced' (S and F) sounds. For example the child must learn that the noun 'house' (unvoiced) becomes the voiced 'housing', and the singular unvoiced 'thief' the plural voiced 'thieves'. Secondly, he must also learn larger features such as those strings of sounds which are likely to occur and strings which are unlikely owing to their being awkward to pronounce. Thus 'sh' is acceptable while 'zh' is unacceptable. But of even greater importance are the prosodic features like the inflection pattern which gives rise to, for example, the rising inflection for a question, and the stress pattern whereby in each word a certain syllable is stressed – change of stress can mark a change in the sentential function of the word so that, for example, the verb órganize is replaced by the noun organizátion.

Studies of phonology tend to be of three kinds: firstly, intensive longitudinal studies of one child; secondly, analysis of data obtained from larger numbers of children to give a statistical picture of 'average' phonological development; and, thirdly, experimental studies designed to test a hypothesis covering a particular aspect of acquisition.

In mastering the segmental features of his language the child has to distinguish both 'types' of sounds, for example nasals or stridents, and members of these types or sets as 'n' versus 'm' or 'f' versus 'v'. The first distinction that the child makes is between vowels and consonants, he then appears to learn an exemplar of a set – 'b' for stops, 'm' for nasals, 'w' for glides – and then to differentiate the other members.

It is possible that the groundwork for this development has been laid during the babbling period when the infant may be able to recognize the differences between sounds and attempt to produce them. Schvachkin (1948) claimed to show that by the age of seventeen months a child is able to distinguish words which differ by only a single phenome (smallest sound unit) and suggested that the schedule of development for phonemic speech perception was universal. While Garnica's (1973) experiments throw doubt on this claim she does say that some general trends are visible and cross-cultural studies (Preston and Yeni-Komshian, 1967) show that children in different linguistic environments produce the same range of speech sounds which do not reflect differences in their respective languages. At first the child seems to reproduce prosodic features and phonemically his words are only approximations to adult speech but as he attempts to make his speech intelligible to those about him so he becomes more accurate in his phonemic production.

At this early stage the child appears incapable of distinguishing and isolating specific sounds in a word, rather he deals with whole words or discrete sound patterns. The Russian psychologist Zhurova (1963) performed a series of experiments on teaching pre-school children to analyse words in terms of single sounds. The children aged three to seven were first shown what was meant by the first sound in a word by finding out the first sound in their own names. They were then asked to play a game and told an elaborate story which was, in summary, that in order to cross a bridge some animals had to give the first sound of their names but, as they could not speak, the child would have to help them by saying it for them. The results showed that initially the children could not understand what was meant by 'the first sound'. During the game they could identify the first sound but not isolate it, rather they produced a kind of stutter, called by the experimenter 'intoning'. When the experimenter herself made use of intonation the child succeeded in isolating the first sound:

Experimenter: Who's coming?
Subject: Doggie
E What's the first sound in your name?

S	D-d-doggie
E	You're not supposed to say the whole word; say only the first sound: d-d-d-
S	D-d-d.

Children of five were more adept at isolating the first sound but they too learnt from the experimenter's intoning when they got into difficulties:

E	Who's coming?
S	Belka (squirrel)
E	What's the first sound in your name?
S	Bel-ka . . . No, not like that . . . Belka . . . How does it go? . . . I can't do it.
E	B-b-belka
S	b-b- right?

The older children, aged six–seven, were also asked to produce the first sounds of the words in the game but did not play the game as such. All these children succeeded without intoning. When asked to isolate the last sound in a word only two of the three to four-year-olds succeeded and that took five to seven demonstrations by the experimenter. Children of four to five could only succeed after intonation and the eldest children performed as the middle group had done in the first experiment. These ingenious experiments show the difficulty experienced by children and suggest that normal development does not require them to isolate specific sounds.

The prosodic features of speech also show a consistent developmental schedule across cultures since the intonational pattern for questions, commands, and statements appears to be similar in different languages. Tonkova Yampol'skaya (1968) set out to answer three questions: does the cry of a newborn infant have any intonational structure?; what are the intonations in the cooing and babbling of infants during the first year of life, and can they be shown to have a communicative value?; and what are the characteristics of the intonational repertoire of infants during the second year? What he found was that speech development in children appears to begin with the development of intonation and that with infants of under six months adults interpreted the meaning of a cry by intonational cues. During the first two years a variety of intonational patterns were developed (fig. 6.1). He concludes that, 'intonation is developed and mastered much earlier than conceptual words and individual sounds' (in Ferguson and Slobin, 1973: 137).

Kaplan (1969) studied infant perception of prosodic features by reading short sentences to the child with either the intonational

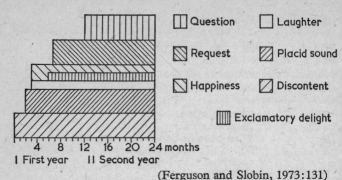

(Ferguson and Slobin, 1973:131)

Fig. 6.1 *Development of intonational forms with age*

pattern of a statement or question or just with a rising or falling voice. While the sentence was being read the infant's heart-rate and general non-verbal behaviour was measured. It was not until eight months that any response was perceived but at eight months it did seem that the infants could distinguish questions from statements. In a more naturalistic study Menyuk and Bernholtz (1969) analysed the spontaneously produced one word utterances of a child and found that the one word was produced with the three distinct intonational patterns of statement, question, and emphatic which suggests that at this stage the child is using the one word to stand for a whole sentence.

During the early years then the child is gradually developing sound and prosodic features until he can both comprehend and produce the phonemic distinctions of his native language and correctly interpret and apply the rules of intonation and stress.

The development of syntax

Broadly speaking language can be divided into two types of linguistic units – phonemes and morphemes (smallest meaningful unit). The morphological structure of language is its word structure, as opposed to its sound structure, and once these words are combined into sentences language can be analysed in terms of syntactic and semantic relations. Syntax covers structure and grammatical relations. What we are concerned with is the extent to which a child, at different stages, understands this structure and the processes by means of which he acquires such knowledge. A problem is that grammatical knowledge can only be inferred from the actual speech, or performance, of a child.

By the age of four or five all children have acquired a knowledge of the major components of the syntactic structure of their native language. The sequence of acquisition appears to be universal although the speed of acquisition will vary from child to child. At the earliest stage the infant seems to be using single words expressing the basic sentential relationships (predicate of the sentence and object of the verb) which are what Chomsky and others consider to be universal relations and are held by him to be innately known by children. In McNeill's (1970b) analysis of Adam's speech he found that most of his early sentences were ones in which the relations expressed were to do with the predicate of the sentence. This, however, is not the only view. Brown, for example, produces the following examples of Adam's utterances: paper find, boy book, part trailer, car mosquito, pencil paper, paper pencil, pencil doggie, (1970b:125), which do not altogether confirm McNeil's statement.

Melissa Bowerman (1973) also argues cogently that it is a mistake to attribute knowledge of grammatical relations to a child on the basis of his early utterances since a close analysis of these utterances shows the evidence for such a claim to be lacking, and this question is still very much under discussion.

Early sentences, however, do seem to have a characteristic structure. Firstly, they appear to be 'telegraphic', that is they are shortened, like telegrams, by leaving out some articles and prepositions, and they contain sequences not heard in adult speech which suggests that the children are applying systematic yet idiosyncratic rules. The description of these sentences as 'telegraphic' is useful but should be used with care since, as Brown (1973) points out, children at this stage frequently use pronouns such as 'I', 'you', 'me', and 'my', and the adjective 'telegraphic' may be too meagre a description, rather the children may be using 'operating principles' as suggested by Slobin (1971) like:

Pay attention to the end of words.
Pay attention to the order of words and morphemes.
Underlying semantic relations should be marked overtly and clearly (Brown, 1973:87).

Children's omissions are not the regular omissions which occur in adult speech, but it would appear that they expect to be understood by familiar adults provided the words used are in some way appropriate. Brown therefore suggests that early speech 'may be said to be well *adapted* to its communicative purpose, well adapted but *narrowly* adapted'. (1973:245)

Secondly, although these utterances have a 'pivot look', the 'open' 'pivot' distinction (Braine 1963) (see p. 96) has been shown to be an inadequate description of the existing data as pivots do occur in isolation and in combination with one another and the children do produce sentences of more than two words. Bloom (1973) suggests that at the earliest stage some children appear to be using a pivot grammar but to describe it as such is too superficial. However, it is perhaps possible to view it as an initial strategy. Nevertheless two and three word combinations are characteristic of this stage and subsequent development occurs by the child's expanding these grammatically simple few word combinations. Limber (1973), who has studied the development of complex sentences found that, firstly, the child modifies a simple noun phrase like 'want hat' to 'want daddy hat' by adding a possessive. Secondly he composes complex sentences by joining two elements, the second of which is known as the 'complement', for example – 'watch the girl feed the ducks' in which 'watch' is the main verb and 'feed the ducks' includes a subordinate verb. In the second year certain conjunctions occur as, 'I don't want you read that book', or 'watch me throw ball'. These sentences are followed by the appearance of adverbs of place, questions, relatives, and conjunctions.

Klima and Bellugi (1966) used the data obtained from Adam, Eve, and Sarah to look at the development of negative and interrogative sentences. Initially, there are no negatives as such but negation is expressed by 'no' or 'not', e.g. 'no the sun shining' or 'no play that'. At a subsequent stage 'don't' and 'can't' appear so that forms such as 'I don't want some supper' and 'I didn't see something' are characteristic. Bloom (1970) refined this analysis by showing that children express three types of negation: first, non-existence; secondly, rejection; and thirdly, denial, and that, developmentally, they appear in this order. Non-existence was finally expressed by 'no more', rejection by 'don't' and denial by 'not', but, initially, while the child was developing a form, for example rejection, he used the form of expression which he had applied to the earlier form, thus rejection would at first be expressed by 'no more' and only later by 'don't'. Cromer comments 'there was strong evidence in Bloom's data then, that cognitive categories of negation developed before the acquisition of linguistic forms to refer to them'. (1974: 217) For interrogative sentences the development is similar with questions first marked by intonation. Children then start to use 'what', 'where' and 'why' as in 'what book name', 'where my mitten' and 'why you waking me up'. Only after this are they able to invert certain verbs for example 'Does the kitty stand up?' and their sentences appear more like adult interrogatives but they do not exhibit the full adult range and still have idiosyncratic forms as 'What did you doed?' and 'How they can't talk?'.

So far we have been concerned with production and not comprehension. Smith *et al* (1970) performed two ingenious experiments which give us some idea of what children attend to. In the first the experimenters were concerned with what constitutes the 'primary linguistic input' for children who are just beginning to speak. They asked thirteen children aged eighteen months to two years to perform certain actions and used commands which were either similar in form to those the children used or those adults used. In addition nonsense words were included in some of the commands of each kind (Table 6A). The results were that, when

Table .6A Free response experimental stimuli

	Structure		
FAMILIARITY	CHILD-FORMS		WELL-FORMED
No nonsense syllables	$n:$ Ball		$vfn:$ Throw me the ball
	$vn:$ Throw ball		
	$Lvn:$ Please Jim, throw ball		
Nonsense syllables	$Xn:$ Gor ball	$vZn:$ Throw ronta ball	
		$Xfn:$ Gor me the ball	
		$XZn:$ Gor ronta ball	

(Ferguson and Slobin, 1973:503)

the group was analysed as a whole, the children were most likely to respond to 'touch commands', that is when they had to touch the object, expressed in the normal adult way, followed by the telegraphic form, with commands including nonsense syllables coming last. However when the analysis separated the more mature from the less mature children it was found that while the more mature were most likely to respond to adult type commands the less mature were more likely to respond to 'telegraphic' ones. When 'attention' responses were analysed, that is, when the children looked at or attended to the objects mentioned by the adult, the pattern was similar, and if the children voluntarily repeated what the adult said they were most likely to repeat sentences which contained nonsense syllables. On the basis of these findings the experimenters concluded that the children seemed to pay attention to those aspects of adult speech which were closest to their own speech and that for younger children comprehension did not differ from performance, but that the older children did appear to comprehend forms which were in advance of what they were themselves producing. There may, therefore, be stages when comprehension is not in advance of production, and others when the child is able to comprehend more complex structures. One could hypothesize that it is necessary for the child to be able to comprehend a structure before he can produce it but if the stucture is too far in advance of his own development it will be ignored.

A second experiment investigated the comprehension of older children, aged three and four, of the structure which they were not producing. The children were simply asked to repeat sentences which varied in grammatical structure, each type was presented in a grammatical and ungrammatical form. They found that certain structures were always easier to repeat and that the children were better at repeating grammatically well formed sentences. The structures were divided into two kinds on the basis of the children's responses: 'A' structures were those which were easier to repeat, and 'B' those which were more difficult. In addition it was noticed that 'A' structures did occur in the children's own speech whereas 'B' structures did not. In repeating ungrammatical sentences of type 'A' the children tended to correct them thereby indicating that they had recognized the structure of the sentence despite the experimenter's error. In 'B' sentences the children had difficulty repeating both the grammatical and the ungrammatical form and did not, in these cases, correct the error. One type of error was interesting and this occurred when the children replied with a simple sentence instead of repeating the complex one they had been given, for example:

Stimulus   The boy who was running fell down.
Response: The boy running fell down.
Stimulus: Mummy could have lost her purse.
Response: Mummy lost her purse.

It would appear that the children attended to those aspects of the sentence which were consonant with their own structure, but this can only be a partial explanation since were they to persist in this they would not develop the more complex structure.

Although by the age of five the child's syntactic competence approximates to that of an adult, development is not at an end. Carol Chomsky (1969) has studied older children's understanding of the verbs 'ask', 'tell', and 'promise', and found that up to about the age of eight children understand the verb 'ask' to mean 'tell'. For example if the child is told, 'tell x what to feed the doll', she

110

will reply 'a banana', but if instead she is told 'ask *x* what to feed the doll' she will again tell the other child and not ask her. However, there was less difficulty when a pronoun was used to draw attention to the subject of the second, embedded, sentence, thus sentences 3 and 4 were easier for the children than sentences 1 and 2:

1 Ask Laura what to feed the doll.
2 Tell Laura what to feed the doll.
3 Ask Laura what you should feed the doll.
4 Tell Laura what she should feed the doll.

Likewise 'promise' was used initially as if it merely meant to 'tell' or 'say' with no notion of obligation. Carol Chomsky suggests that children may not have fully acquired the syntactic rules until nine years of age. But Limber (1973) points out that in dealing with verbs of this kind the child does not in fact have to acquire a new rule so much as recognize these verbs as exceptions to rules which he has already acquired. These verbs violate the 'minimal distance principle' which says the subject of the verb in the second, embedded, sentence should be as near as possible:

1 The mother paid her daughter to sweep the room.
2 The mother promised her daughter to sweep the room.
3 The mother asked her daughter to sweep the room.
4 The mother asked her daughter which room to sweep.

In sentence 1 the subject of 'to sweep' is 'daughter' whereas in sentence 2 it is 'mother' which shows how 'promise' violates the 'minimal distance principle'. But 'ask' is sometimes exceptional and sometimes not, in 3 it obeys the principle and in 4 violates it. Since children master 'promise' before 'ask' it is easier, as Slobin (1972) points out, for them to learn a consistent rather than an inconsistent exception.

Semantic development

Descriptions of language acquisition which are restricted to syntactic considerations have been described as 'inadequate', not because they are necessarily incorrect but because they appear 'lean' in comparison with the 'richer' interpretations which include semantic features (Brown 1973). Semantics is the study of meaning and therefore the study of semantic development is the investigation of how a child learns to comprehend and produce meanings. In order to develop language as a vehicle for meaning the child has both to learn the meanings of individual words and the way semantic roles such as agent or object acted upon are expressed in a sentence. To know the difference between the subject and object of a sentence is to be aware of their grammatical relationships but to distinguish the agent from the object acted upon is to be aware of their semantic roles. Several theorists have recently concentrated on the child's semantic intentions and knowledge since they argue that in order to know how to use a word the child must first know what it means and hence an understanding of semantic development is basic to understanding language acquisition.

Melissa Bowerman has argued that 'children's initial efforts at word combination result from their discovery of ways to express various semantic relationships in the language they are learning' (1973:210). For her the expression of semantic relations preceeds any understanding of grammatical relations since she maintains that over time 'a child may begin to recognize similarities in the way different semantic concepts are formally dealt with and to gradually reorganize his knowledge according to the more abstract grammatical relationships which are functional in the particular language he is learning'. (1973:213) In support of this view she considers first word combinations and shows that in Gvozdev's (1961) study of Zhenya, Zhenya initially only singled out certain direct objects, namely a small group which represented the objects acted upon. This would suggest that she had developed the semantic category of 'object acted upon' before the more general syntactic category of 'object' since if the syntactic category of object were developed first she should have singled out all objects as being syntactically equivalent and not just a small group. In addition she found that the first verbs used most frequently by children were those verbs which had an active subject, thus: *sleep*, *drive*, *eat*, *sit*, *sing*, *ride*, *go*, and *open* were frequent whereas *want*, *see*, and *feel* which take as subjects 'persons affected' or 'object involved' were infrequent.

Similarly Bloom (1970) has stressed the importance of semantic intentions by pointing out that the two word utterance 'mummy sock' can either mean that the sock belongs to the mother or that the mother is putting on the child's sock. Here a single surface structure can express two distinct deep semantic structures. Bloom studied three children in considerable depth and found that their two word noun plus noun combinations could express five distinct semantic relationships underlying a single surface structure. Following Chomsky she proposed a description of child language which involves a deep semantic structure which is transformed into the observable surface structure. Schlesinger (1971) differs from Bloom in bypassing the deep structure by positing 'semantic level'. He maintains that before a sentence can be produced a person must intend to say something which is meaningful. Only after this intention is present is a sentence constructed which best expresses the intended meaning. This initial intention is to do with concepts and relations and is therefore part of a child's cognitive capacity. Thus the concept of agent and object must precede the choice of words which express a notion such as agency. If this is so what the child has to learn initially are the rules for transforming his intentions into his native language and how to realize his intentions in language. The child therefore begins from the semantic features of utterances and learns the structural rules by being exposed to a series of instances of their usage, for example if he hears 'Catherine sock' 'daddy hat' etc., since he already knows that Catherine and daddy are people and socks and shoes are objects and that these sentences represent a relationship between the two he comes to develop the possessive relation of person plus object. Thus it is the semantic concepts which are the 'primitive structural components of sentences'. (Bowerman, 1973:199)

Conceptually it seems reasonable to argue that semantic intentions or a concern for meaning must proceed the syntactic realization of these meanings and confidence is strengthened in this type of argument by Brown's finding that when he analysed the speech of twelve children studied in various countries he found that there exists a short list of semantic relations which will account for the majority of stage 1 utterances produced by twelve unacquainted children learning four different languages. (1973:182) These relations he lists as:

1 Agent and action
2 Action and object
3 Agent and object
4 Action and locative or location
5 Entity and locative or location
6 Possessor and possession
7 Entity and attributive
8 Demonstrative and entity (1973:173)

So far we have been concerned with semantic functions of words but another area of interest is one explored by Eve Clark (1973a) and this is the way in which words are used to refer to external objects and events. She argues that when a child first uses a word he is ignorant of its full adult meaning and may use it in too limited a sense or too widely. In this case semantic development means the development of the adult meaning of words. This is illustrated by some very early data on restructuring (Pavlovitch,

Table 6.B The restructuring of a semantic domain[a]

	Word(s)	Semantic domain
Stage I	bébé	reflection of self in mirror; photo of self; all photos; all pictures; books with pictures; all books
Stage II	(a) bébé	reflection of self in mirror; photo of self; all pictures; books with pictures
	(b) deda [grandfather]	all photos
Stage III	(a) bébé	reflection of self in mirror; photo of self; books with pictures; all books
	(b) deda	all photos
	(c) ka'ta [karta = card]	all pictures of landscapes' views
Stage IV	(a) bébé	reflection of self in mirror; photo of self
	b) deda	all photos
	(c) ka'ta	all pictures (not of people)
	(d) kiga [book]	all books
Stage V	(a) bébé	self; small children in pictures
	(b) deda	photos
	(c) ka'ta	pictures
	(d) kiga	books
	(e) slika [reflection]	reflections in mirror
	(f) duda [Douchau, own name]	photo of self

[a]Data from Pavlovitch (1920).

(Timothy E. Moore (ed.), 1973)

1920) (Table 6.B). Clark suggests that the earliest word meanings may be derived from the infant's perceptual abilities. Ervin-Tripp (1966) also finds that first nouns used refer to things which have characteristic sizes and visual contours, likewise the first verbs are verbs of movement either human or animal. These views relate to Brown's comment that stage I functional meanings may be derived from sensori-motor intelligence in that 'Piaget's description of the time when each thing is conceived by the child in terms of the scheme into which he can enter, as 'graspable', 'suckable', 'scratchable' and so on, is irresistibly suggestive of lexical entries for nouns and verbs which describe combinations into which they can enter'. (1973:200) He concludes that 'the first sentences explore the construction of reality which is the terminal achievement of sensori-motor intelligence'. (1973:200)

All of the studies just mentioned are comparatively recent, the findings tentative, and perhaps when explored in detail confusing, but Halliday's (in press) picture of one child's 'learning how to mean' makes the abstract argument more concrete and comprehensible. He is concerned with how a child learns the system of meanings and points out that 'meaningful expression' can exist before words if the child's sounds are interpreted functionally, that is in terms of use. What the child has to do is to transform these vestigial sound usages into a fully developed adult system and Halliday sees this development as falling into phases. One phase consists of the child's initial functional linguistic system; another, the transition from this system to that of the adult language; and another, the learning of the adult language (p. 5).

All Halliday's data was obtained from the intensive study of a single child, Nigel, between the ages of nine and twenty-four months. At the very first stage, ten and a half months, Nigel had no grammar as such but did make sounds which could be interpreted as having four specific uses: (1) Instrumental – a demand (2) Regulatory – or manipulative (3) Interactional, both friendly and impatient, and (4) Personal, showing withdrawal and participation. This phase was continued until sixteen and a half months and during this time Nigel increased the range of his usages. A young child can use language to express his needs and wants (Instrumental); to effect the behaviour of others (Regulatory); to interact with others (Interpersonal); and to express his awareness of himself (Personal). The Heuristic function refers to the child's ability to explore that which is not himself in contrast with the Personal and the Imaginative use of language which leads to the creation of a possible world as distinct from the actual world. The Informative function, of course, means to use language to give information.

In the next phase Nigel developed a grammar and vocabulary, that is his earlier expressions of meaning became words, either singly or together, which acted as the vehicles for meanings. Initially one word related to one function 'cat' meant 'hello cat' (Interactional) (p. 11), but he soon began to produce two functions in one sentence, for example 'cake' meaning 'look there is a cake and I want some' (page 11). As Nigel learnt more about his environment so he used more words to express what he was seeing and to recall what he had seen but not, at this stage, in the sense of sharing an experience with another. What he did appear to be doing was to combine the phase 1 Personal and Heuristic functions into a 'learning function' by means of which he was attempting to make sense of his environment. This function is called by Halliday the 'Mathetic' and was seen in the typical question 'what's that?' or the statement 'that are . . .'. At the same time as the 'Mathetic' function was apparent, Nigel also showed a 'Pragmatic' function which was a combination of the phase 1 Instrumental and Regulatory functions. The difference between these two functions was signalled by Nigel, from the age of nineteen months, using a rising tone for the Pragmatic function and a falling tone for the Mathetic one. These two functions were initially expressed by two distinct structures, for example 'more meat' or 'mend train' was always used Pragmatically and 'green car', 'two books' was always Mathetic. It is only later that the 'more x' structure could be used to mean 'look there is some more x' rather than 'give me more x', and likewise 'green car' would mean 'I want the green car' as well as 'look there's a green car', but, initially, the rule seemed to be one structure, one function. Thus with the appearance of simple structures and words Nigel exhibited a level between meaning and sound and it is this level which would subsequently become adult grammar.

This phase was also characterized by the emergence of dialogue. In phase 1 he could express the meaning 'yes and no' in the sense of 'yes I want that', 'no I don't want that' (Instrumental) or 'yes do that', 'no don't do that' (Regulatory), but he had no general polarity (positive/negative) system, nor could he respond to any questions seeking information, such as 'did you see a car?' or 'what did you see?' Before he is able to engage in dialogue the child has not only to be aware of roles as such but of specifically linguistic roles as the addresser and the addressee. Within the two weeks between eighteen and eighteen and a half months Nigel learnt to respond to *wh* questions, to a command, to a statement, to a response, and initiate dialogue in the limited sense of asking 'what's that'. Having begun to engage in dialogue Nigel was able to develop the social role of language and to use language in his environmental explorations. Phase 2 therefore was transitional in two senses, firstly the development of grammar and dialogue marked the transition from phase 1 to the adult language system, and, secondly, it was transitional between the employment of discrete functions where function equalled use, and the adult abstract sense of function as objective or subjective, ideational or interpersonal (see p. 102) since Halliday had shown that Nigel's initial functions were collapsed in phase 2 into the Pragmatic or Mathetic functions, marked by the use of a rising tone for the former and a falling tone for the latter, and that it was this binary division which formed a basis for the adult functional distinction.

7
Influences on language acquisition

In considering the acquisition of language it is clear that the similarities between children are more striking than the differences. Nevertheless, any outline, however brief, of language acquisition would be incomplete without reference to the magnitude, nature, and causes of individual differences in language use and hence, by implication, of the various influences on language acquisition. Language is a social phenomenon and Halliday (in press) in his detailed and theoretically illuminating study of Nigel highlights this when he says:

> If, for example, language is used from an early stage, to regulate the behaviour of others and it is suggested that the mastery of this function is one of the essential steps of the developmental process, this assumes some general framework of social structure and social processes in terms of which a function such as 'regulatory' would make sense. More particularly – since we are concerned with the language of a child – it presupposes a concept of cultural transmission within which the role of language in the transmission process may be highlighted and defined. Here the concept of meaning, and of learning to mean, is in the last analysis interpreted in sociological terms, in the context of some chain of dependence such as: social order – transmission of a social order to the child – role of language in the transmission process – functions of language in relation to his role (p. 4).

Therefore we must not neglect the context in which language is acquired since this will both affect the range of linguistic experiences to which the child is exposed and the nature of his production. It was found (Campbell and Wales, 1970) that children use comparative expressions more frequently in a competitive situation when they were comparing their performance with that of other children (in, for example, building sand-castles), than in a situation when a comparative element was lacking. Thus the presence or absence of certain linguistic forms in a child's speech may be more a function of a situation in which the speech is produced than of the child's competence. Such situations can be set up experimentally and the child's competence inferred from the usages elicited. For example, when a group of nursery school children were shown a series of cardboard soldiers which varied in height and were questioned about them, the result showed that in this situation the children were able to produce absolutes 'he's big', comparatives 'he's bigger than him', and superlatives 'he's the biggest soldier'. (Campbell and Wales, 1970)

Parental influence

To think of a child as acquiring language in a certain context immediately raises the question of the significance of the parents. How important are parents in facilitating or retarding the speech of their children? Indeed, how influential are they? The manner in which parents speak to their children differs from that which they use with adults. When studying the speech of a mother to her two-year-old, Dracht *et al* (1969) found that she spoke in grammatically simple short sentences, many of which were repeated. Slobin (1972) reports that the mothers in Roger Brown's Harvard study seem to simplify their speech so that it differed little from the speech of some five-year-old black children studied by Kernan. In other words a two-year-old child, whether in Brown's or Kernan's sample, was being exposed to a similar linguistic input but in the first case its source was the child's mother and the second his five-year-old peers.

In addition to using a restricted form of speech mothers do attempt to expand their children's utterances by repeating them in a more grammatical form, for example 'mummy sandwich' was expanded 'mummy will have a sandwich' and 'pick glove' to 'pick the glove up' (Brown and Bellugi, 1964). The problem here is whether the parental expansion is related to what the child intended to say, since in the first instance the child may really have meant that he wanted to hold or look at his mother's sandwich. However, failure on the part of an adult or parent to understand may be helpful. When one of the children studied in Edinburgh said 'Isn't a torch got a battery not as different as that?' and the experimenters said 'Eh?' and the child replied 'Isn't a battery in a torch not the same as that?'. (Campbell and Wales, 1970)

Cazden (1965) compared three groups of two and a half-year-old working-class children in a nursery school. One group received no special linguistic training; the second group spent one hour a day five days a week for three months with an adult who expanded everything they said; and the third 'modelling' group spent the same time with an adult as the expansion group but in their case the adult commented on the content of their utterances rather than expanding them. For example, if the child said 'boy cry' the adult would say 'yes, he's sad'. The result showed that although the expansion group did show slightly more linguistic improvement than the control group the 'modelling' group improved most of all. It is possible that expanding everything the child said gave the child more information than he could cope with or, again, expansion might have been more useful if the experimenter had expanded in a way that was only one stage beyond the child's competence rather than expanding all his sentences, which introduce many different degrees of linguistic complexity. When Feldman and Rodgon (1970) performed a similar experiment but divided expansion into 'contingent' and 'non-contingent' (where the former meant that only clear utterances were expanded and the latter that all utterances were expanded), they found that 'contingent' expansions were more effective than 'non-contingent', and that both kinds were more effective than modelling.

Slobin (1964) studied what he called 'imitation of expansions', which occurred when a mother made a statement and the child repeated part of it, which was then followed by the mother repeating the statement correctly and the child again attempting to imitate part of this. Alternatively the same thing could occur when the child made a statement, the mother expanded it, and the child attempted to imitate part of her expansions. For example:

Mother: 'Would you like some cake?'
Child: 'Like cake'
Mother: 'Yes, would you like some cake?'

Slobin found that mothers expanded about 30 per cent of the time and the children imitated 10 per cent of the time. Some of these imitations were in advance of what they produced but the number of such advanced imitations were too small to base any firm conclusions on it. In a study of three children Cazden (1968) found that the child who received fewer expansions was relatively the most advanced in the acquisition of noun and verb inflections.

Expansion then seems to have little facilitative effect but perhaps direct attempts to improve a child's speech would meet with more success. Brown and Hanlon (1970) looked at the aspects of the child's speech which were commented on by parents and found that parents were not concerned with whether the child's sentences were grammatically well or ill formed, but were concerned with whether what the child said was true or false. Their only linguistic corrections appeared to be of pronunciations, 'naughty words', or forms like 'digged' or 'goed' (Brown, 1973). Indeed when parents do attempt to correct grammar directly they seem to have little effect. McNeill quotes the following conversation:

Child: 'Nobody don't like me'
Mother: 'No, say "nobody likes me" '
Child: 'Nobody don't like me'
(This exchange was repeated eight times)
Mother: 'No, now listen carefully say "nobody likes me" '
Child: 'Oh! nobody don't likes me' (1966:69)

However, Dodd (1972) showed that when parents stimulated their children aged between nine and twelve months vocal stimulation alone had no effect but vocal and social stimulations increased the quantity of babbling. It did not, however, alter the type of sounds the children made, in other words they did not imitate the sounds their parents made but merely increased quantitatively the production of their own sounds.

Imitation also seems to have little significance for a child's acquisition of words. Ricks (1972) found that early words were of two types. Firstly, 'dadda' words which were related to babbling and did not refer in any particular way to distinct objects or people; and, secondly, 'label' words which did have reference but which were often made up by the children themselves. In his experiment three types of tapes were played to the children. The first was composed of 'dadda' words, the second of 'label' words, and the third of a meaningless series of sounds which the children could have produced but which had not in fact appeared. There were some imitations by the children of all three tapes but imitation of the made-up strings was low, whereas the highest number of imitations were in response to the 'label' words. The child, therefore, seems to imitate what he is producing more than new words and it is possible that the impetus for the production of new words is not their being heard, so much as the child's awareness of an object or person that he wishes to label.

It does not appear that children develop syntactic structure through directly imitating their parents' syntax. In an early study Fraser, Bellugi, and Brown (1963) looked at imitation, comprehension, and production. In this experiment using children aged thirty-seven to forty-three months there were three experimental conditions. In the first, the comprehension condition, the experimenter showed the child two pictures (fig. 7.1) and said 'the sheep are jumping' and 'the sheep is jumping'. He then repeated one sentence and asked the child to point to the picture which depicted the situation described in the sentence that had just been repeated. In the second, the imitation condition, there were no pictures. The experimenter merely said the two sentences 'the

(adapted from Oldfield and Marshall, 1968:124)

Fig. 7.1 *Pictures illustrating a grammatical contrast: left 'the sheep is jumping'; right 'the sheep are jumping'*

sheep is walking' and 'the sheep are walking' and the child was asked to repeat each sentence after the experimenter. In the third, the production condition, the experimenter again showed two pictures and named them, that is repeated the sentence which correctly described the situation. He then pointed to one picture and asked the child to name it. Ten grammatical contrasts were used. The results showed that imitation preceeded both comprehension and production and comprehension preceeded production, so that in this experiment imitation appeared as a form of parroting.

It could, however, be argued that to ask a child to imitate directly may not be as informative as studying the spontaneous imitations which occur when a child is speaking with an adult. Ervin compared two-year-old children's spontaneous imitations with the same children's spontaneous free speech and found that the level of grammatical correctness was the same for both. In other words children did not imitate grammatical forms which were more complex or more advanced than those which occurred in their own speech. Thus when she wrote a grammar for the free speech and the imitations she found that the two were similar. What the children did do when imitating was to select the recent and most emphasized word and preserved the word order of the adult original. She concludes:

If we can rely at all on this sample of five children there is an

121

inescapable conclusion. Imitations under the optimal conditions, those of immediate recall, are not grammatically progressive. We cannot look to overt imitation as a source for the rapid progress children make in grammatical scale in these early years.

A word of caution, I have *not* said that imitation is never important in language learning. In comprehension, overt imitation may be important. Possibly imitation aids in the acquisition of a vocabulary or phonetic mastery. Perhaps overt imitation is indispensable in the special conditions of classroom language learning. All I have said is that there is not a shred of evidence supporting a view that progress towards adult norms and grammar arises merely from practice in overt imitations of adult sentences. (1964:172)

Parents do, however, switch codes when speaking to their children, and this aspect of language acquisition whereby the child learns the correct code to use when addressing parents, playmate, or authority figure has been largely ignored by researchers. It is nevertheless an important element. Berko-Gleason studied spontaneous speech in five families, with one four-year-old child studied in most detail and in a variety of situations, for example at nursery school or playing with the author's eight-year-old daughter. She found that adults had two distinct codes, firstly a 'baby talk style' consisting in a higher tone of voice; expansion of the child's expressions; simple sentences, composed of concrete nouns, diminutives, and terms of affection. Berko-Gleason remarks 'one mother . . . spoke in a normal voice to her husband, a high voice to her four-year-old, a raised voice to her eight-year-old, and when she talked to her baby she fairly squeaked' (1963:161). With children aged four to eight, while terms of affection or nicknames remained, expansions were replaced by either actual or implied imperatives, and the language was used in a more regulatory socializing way. Parents also tended to include more in their speech than they would with an adult so if they asked a question they also gave the answer; 'Where's your lunch box? I bet it's inside' (1963:162). There was also a considerable degree of exaggeration of response as when a mother, on being shown some old toys her child had been given, 'whooped with joy'. Berko-Gleason comments that it is as if the parents were showing the child how he ought to feel.

Even the youngest children showed some variation in code; this was that they spoke to their family and kept silent when strangers were present. Children under four also exhibited a 'selective use of whining' (1963:163) by changing to a whining tone when a parent appeared although they had been speaking in an ordinary way before. The children did not employ a formal style, but when one four-year-old was explaining to the experimenters that he would put his tooth under his pillow and get a present from the fairy who would take the tooth away, his style was more narrative and didactic than that which he used to his parents or peers. When speaking to peers the children use more noises and expletives like 'yakk' or 'blech' than with adults and they used no terms of affection. They would also repeat what another child had said which is interesting in the light of research findings related to their imitations of adult speech (see p. 120). One example of this was the following exchange between three nursery school children:

Sue: 'Well, don't you want to see the raspberries?'
Malcolm: 'How 'bout you pick some for me and I'll eat
           them?'
Eric: 'Yeah, and how 'bout you pick some for me and
           I'll eat them?' (1963:165)

Eight-year-olds but not four-year-olds appeared to be able to use baby talk to the youngest children. Six-year-olds tried but were not able to modify their language sufficiently for it to be true baby talk. Berko-Gleason remarks that baby talk is not remembered but has to be re-learnt and the young children, whose use of language was still developing, 'made their sentences the only way they knew how, grinding them out with laborious intensity at times, looking neither to the baby left nor formal right'. (1963:166)

Therefore, parents do modify their speech both grammatically and stylistically when speaking to their children but there is, as yet, little evidence that this has any significant effect on the rate at which their children acquire either syntactic or stylistic aspects of language.

Cognitive influences

If children, then, do not appear to be influenced by their parents, what aspects of speech do they attend to? Word order would seem to be important but some particularly interesting suggestions are made in Eve Clark's paper *How Children Describe Time and Order* (1973). She points out that adults can express the same idea in different ways and suggests three principles which can determine how an adult chooses to describe temporal events. Firstly, it is simpler to mention events in the same order as they actually happened, for example 'he came in, he sat down, and he opened the paper'. People appear to prefer a sentence in which order of mention and chronological order are the same rather than one in which they are inverted. Secondly, one sentence will be chosen in preference to another if it has 'derivational simplicity', that is if there are fewer transformations between its deep and surface structure. The third principle is choice of theme: Clark explained that 'any communication in English is organized in *theme* and *rheme*. The theme is the first member of a sentence and is the "subject" of the utterance, the rheme comprises the information given about the theme'. (1973:590) Therefore, whatever the speaker chooses as the theme determines what will be mentioned first. The child, then, may begin by following the 'order of mention' principle but once he has learnt about theme he may have to depart from that in order to focus attention on his theme. Then 'he ate and he left' becomes 'he left after he ate' since this construction allows the child to use his leaving as the theme with 'when he left' as the rheme. Clark therefore hypothesized the following stages of development:

1 the child uses short sentences, describing the events in chronological order.
2 he uses co-ordinate clauses, still describing the events in chronological order.
3 he recognises, at some time prior to (4), that the order theme/rheme is the usual one in English.
4 he develops an alternative to the co-ordinate clause construction for when he is describing events out of chronological order. This involves a main clause followed by a subordinate clause. At first, the conjunction may be omitted.
5 after the conjunctions are freely used in (4), the contingency relation between the events is recognized, much as the theme was in (3).
6 the subordinate clause is used in first position so that the order of mention again corresponds with chronological order, as in (1) and (2). (1973:592)

Clark studied the spontaneous utterances of children aged three and a half in an Edinburgh nursery school and found that the hypothesized schedule was confirmed. The child's choice of one form of expression rather than another did appear to be a function of the interaction of these three principles. Clark's observations could be an explanation of one of Brown's findings (see page 121), that when children had to name one or two pictures by repeating the sentences describing it, (the production condition), they tended to choose the correct picture but instead of repeating 'the woman gives a bunny the teddy' they said 'the woman gives the teddy to the bunny' which is simpler as order of mention and chronological order coincide. When asked to imitate the sentence,

124

however, they did not transform it in this way, presumably because, as Brown suggests, the imitation tasks 'did not work through the meaning system' (1963:67).

It therefore appears that children do pay attention to some aspects of the language they hear but that these aspects are more to do with meaning than structure, it is as if the structures develop to express their meanings and hence attempts to expand or correct structure will fail if the new structure does not appear to the child to represent a more adequate way of expressing his meanings. This would appear to account for both Cazden's finding that 'modelling', that is expansion of content, had more effect on grammatical development than direct grammatical expansion (see p. 119) and for McNeill's intransigent child who was clearly concerned with the negative meaning she was trying to express and was not yet aware that two negatives do not double the negative impact (p. 120).

Class influences

A child's linguistic competence, although somewhat affected by context, seems to develop in a consistent fashion: it is shaped by the child's taking in what he can and only changing when he is ready and the change seems necessary to him. However communicative competence and to a lesser degree linguistic competence do show the influence of both culture and class. These factors may be more related to stylistic than to syntactic or semantic components but at times all three become intermingled. When children from a specific social group speak in a way that is typical of that group we can assume that their ability to learn is unimpaired. Indeed children who speak non-standard English may have to learn more than standard speakers since syntactic development contains generalized if not universal characteristics and therefore the child may have to unlearn a standard form which he had previously developed.

To consider the influence of social class on language acquisition, is to enter the realm of sociolinguistics rather than that of psycholinguistics; however psychologists cannot afford to neglect evidence from other disciplines if their findings are to form part of a coherent whole. Bernstein distinguishes two types of code, the 'elaborated' and the 'restricted'. These codes can be defined on a linguistic level, in terms of the probability of predicting for any one speaker which syntactic elements will be used to organize meaning. In the case of an elaborated code, the speaker will select from a relatively extensive range of alternatives and therefore the probability of predicting the pattern of organizing elements is considerably reduced. In the case of a restricted code the number of these alternatives is often severely limited and the probability of predicting the pattern is greatly increased. (1971:76–77) A restricted code is to do with particular meanings and can be learned in an informal setting, but an elaborated code gives access to universal meanings and requires both formal and informal opportunities for learning. The restricted code is associated with the lower working-class group, or lower-income group, and the elaborated code with the middle class, although the middle class can, as the occasion requires, use both codes. Bernstein tested the degree of association between class and code by looking at the phenomena of hesitation, since greater verbal planning was thought to be indicated by an increased use of pauses. To do this he selected a middle-class and a working-class group and analysed a section of each boy's speech during a free discussion. The findings were that, independent of intelligence, the working-class boys paused less, had longer phrases, and used shorter words. Differences in grammatical elements in the utterances of the members of the two groups were then analysed and he found that there were considerable differences in grammatical usage. These results, he suggests, do support the hypothesis that 'the different class groups are differently orientated in their structural and lexicon choices'. (1971:109)

The findings of this and other experiments suggest that there is an association between class and code and that codes have distinguishing characteristics. It is important that Bernstein should not be misunderstood on this point since he is studying actual speech not the underlying rules of language, considering the relationship between speech and its role as that which both realizes and regulates social relations, and is concerned, like Clark (1973) (see page 123), with 'a study of rules, formal and informal, which regulate the options which we take up in the various contexts in which we find ourselves' (1971:173), that is, all speech codes must comply with linguistic rules but which code is used is a function of class.

Bernstein is interested in the effect different types of social relationships have on speech. Restricted social relationships, in which meanings are mutually available, only require a restricted code; elaboration in this context is unnecessary. When, however, there is a difference between the participants in an exchange it is necessary for them to use more elaborate forms to explicate meaning together with a certain amount of redundancy. The speaker has both to appreciate the difference between his viewpoint and that of the listener and adapt his speech accordingly. A group of middle-class and working-class children were shown a series of four pictures which together illustrated a story and the children were asked to tell the story. The middle-class children's stories could be understood without the pictures being present whereas those of the working-class children were more tied to the particular pictorial stimulus and would not have been comprehensible without the illustrations. The middle-class children were also constrained but in a different way. When they were asked 'what is the man saying?' they replied 'I don't know' and would only role-play when the question was put hypothetically as 'what do you think the man might be saying?'. Working-class children were willing to role-play in response to the first question. Therefore the middle-class children were asking that others elaborate their meanings since they wished to be quite clear what was required before they would commit themselves. Bernstein accounts for these differences by distinguishing four significant socializing contexts, namely:

(1) the regulative context – these are authority relationships where the child is made aware of the rules of the moral order and their various backings. (2) the instructional context, where the child learns about the objective nature of objects and persons and acquires skills of various kinds. (3) the imaginative or innovative context, where the child is encouraged to experiment and recreate his world on his own terms, and in his own way. (4) the interpersonal context, where the child is made aware of affective states – his own, and others. (1971:181)

He then says that if in these contexts the linguistic means of socializing are restricted the result will be that the child develops a restricted code and if they are elaborated then an elaborated code will be developed.

A series of studies by Bernstein and his co-workers Brandis and Henderson (1970) suggest that it is the way a mother interacts with her child that affects linguistic usage rather than any clear one to one correspondence between, for example, maternal expansions and syntactic development. To measure a mother's style of interaction they developed an instrument called the 'Index of Communication and Control'. This was a measure of a mother's typical response, as assessed by a questionnaire and interviews, to everyday situations (Table 7.A). Bernstein describes the qualitative dimensions by saying

a mother with a high score on the Index of Communication and Control is disposed to speak frequently with her child, to pro-

Table 7.A Maternal Index contents

| | Mother is disposed towards: | |
Situation	Low Score	High Score
Child asks a difficult question	Evasion	Cognitive Verbal Interaction
Child talks	Constraint	Verbal Interaction
Child misbehaves (punishment)	Constraint	Absence of constraint
Child misbehaves (Child-oriented reasoning)	Absence of Cognitive Verbal Interaction	Cognitive Verbal Interaction
Uses of Toys	(Instrumental) Mother-Orientation	Cognitive Child-Orientation

(Brandis and Henderson, 1970:145)

mote occasions in which speech is appropriate, to elaborate verbally reasons and rules, and she is concerned to develop her child's active understanding. A mother with a Low Index score is more disposed to limit or discourage verbal interaction, to use physical coercion with her child and to place a weaker emphasis on language in the moral and cognitive aspect of socialisation. (1971:145)

Bernstein and Brandis looked at:

the associations between the more developed Index of Communication and Control and parental social class, family size, ordinal position of the child, sex of the child, ability and W.I.S.C. [Weschler Intelligence Scale for Children] scores of the child *and* the associations between the Index and the nature of the boundary the mothers drew between themselves and the school, the potential disagreements between the mothers and the school and the teachers' estimates of the children's future school career. (1971:93)

Their results are complex but, in summary, they found that within the middle-class group high ability in the child was not related to the mother's Maternal Index score but that within the working-class group was, whereas within the middle-class group a high Maternal Index score was related to more elaborated speech in the children. Less able working-class children appeared to receive less maternal support and encouragement than did their middle-class counterparts; middle-class mothers were also more responsive to a wider range of their children's behaviours but there was a form of sexual discrimination in that middle-class girls were socialized into a more submissive role with less encouragement to excel intellectually. An interesting finding was the high relationship between a working-class mother's score and the teachers' assessment of the child's performance at school: the children of mothers with high scores, regardless of their ability, were consistently rated more highly by their teachers.

Hess and Shipman had followed a similar line of thought since their initial position was:

first, that the behaviour which leads to social, educational, and economic poverty is socialized in early childhood: second, that the central quality involved in the effects of cultural deprivation is a lack of cognitive meaning in the mother/child communication system: and, third, that the growth of cognitive processes is fostered in family control systems which offer and permit a wide range of alternatives of action and thought and that such growth is constricted by systems of control which offer predetermined solutions and few alternatives for consideration and choice. (1963:869)

They looked at a group of 140 black mothers and their four-year-old children who came from four distinct levels of social status. The focus of their concern was the childrens' orientation towards learning as a result of maternal methods of communication and interaction. Two aspects of learning were studied. On the one hand they contrasted an assertive initiatory approach to learning with a passive compliant mode, and on the other they compared the tendency to reach solutions impetuously with a more reflective, evaluative approach. They then taught certain tasks to the mothers and asked them to teach the same tasks to their children. What they found was that the style of teaching differed significantly on class lines. These differences are best illustrated by actual quotations recorded while the mothers were attempting to teach their child how to sort a group of toys:

Mother A: 'All right, Susan, this board is the place where we put the little toy: first of all you're supposed to learn how to place them according to colour. Can you do that? These things that are all the same colour you put in one section; in a second section you put another group of colours and in the third section you put the last group of colours. Can you do that? Would you like to see me do it first?'
Child: 'I want to do it.'
Mother B: 'Now, I'll take them all off the board: now you put them all back on the board. What are these?'.

129

Child:	'A truck'.
Mother:	'All right, just put them right here: put the other one right here: all right, put the other one there.'
Mother C:	'I've got some chairs and cards, do you want to play the game?'

(Child does not respond)

Mother:	'Okay. What's this?'
Child:	'A wagon.'
Mother:	'Hm?'
Child:	'A wagon?'
Mother:	'This is not a wagon. What's this?' (1963:881–882)

Affectively the mothers did not differ, that is all four groups showed a similar level of affection and concern, but verbally and cognitively they did in that the higher status mothers were more likely to explain the task and give the child a structure within which he could work; they were also more reflective. The experimenters conclude:

> the picture that is beginning to emerge is that the meaning of deprivation is the deprivation of meaning – a cognitive environment in which behaviour is controlled by status rules rather than by attention to the individual characteristics of a specific situation and one in which behaviour is not mediated by verbal cues or by teaching that relates events to one another and the present to the future. (1963:885)

The above studies have concentrated on mother/child interaction but since the child learns how to use language within the context of the family Bernstein's theories of the influence of the family structure on the type of codes selected is of interest. He distinguishes between families in terms of the strength of their 'boundary maintaining procedures' (1971:184). In some families, 'positional' families, each member's role is clearly defined and hence the home is tightly organized; in 'person centred' families, however, the emphasis is on the qualities of the individual members. In the latter case the fluidity of the situation requires more discussion and reference to personal feelings, intentions, and desires which will affect the language used. In the 'positional' family an elaborated code would be more likely to refer to objects and in a 'personal' family to persons, however a restricted code is more likely to occur in 'positional' families where the meaning system is less ambiguous and hence needs less elaboration.

Influences on language acquisition are difficult to disentangle but the common assumption that child language is almost wholly the result of parental influence can be seen to be false. In terms of the development of linguistic competence parents appear to have little influence in comparison with the significance of the meanings the child wishes to express. However, in terms of how the child elects to use this competence we can see that class does affect production, as clearly so too may function, context and code.

In summary it seems as if linguistically superficial but sociologically central factors are the most amenable to external influence and it is for the psychologist or the educationalist to weigh the significance of the linguistic versus the sociological features when deciding whether intervention in the form of 'enrichment programmes' is necessary. All children develop linguistic competence; whether their communicative performance is or is not consonant with that of members of another group, is, in the author's opinion, no reason for imputing language deficit: and indeed to do so would seem to demonstrate an ignorance of what constitutes linguistic competence.

Further Reading

Baldwin, Alfred L. (1967) *Theories of Child Development*. New York: John Wiley and Sons.

Beard, Ruth Mary (1969) *An Outline of Piaget's Developmental Psychology for Students and Teachers*. New York: Basic Books.

Bernstein, B. (1971) *Theoretical Studies towards a Sociology of Language*. Vol. 1 of *Class, codes and control*. London: Routledge and Kegan Paul.

Bower, T. G. R. (1974) *Development in Infancy*. San Francisco: W. H. Freeman.

Boyle, D. G. (1969) *A Student's Guide to Piaget*. Elmsford, New York: Pergamon Press.

Bruner, Jerome S. (1973) *Beyond the Information Given*. London: George Allen and Unwin.

Bruner, Jerome S., Olver, Rose R., and Greenfield, Patricia M. (1966) *Studies in Cognitive Growth*. New York: John Wiley and Sons.

Brown, Roger (1973) *A First Language*. London: George Allen and Unwin.

Bryant, Peter (1974) *Perception and Understanding in Young Children*. London: Methuen.

Elkind, D. (1970) *Children and Adolescents: Interpretative Essays on Jean Piaget*. New York: Oxford University Press.

Ferguson, Charles A. and Slobin, Dan I. (eds.) (1973) *Studies of Child Language Development*. New York: Holt, Rinehart and Winston.

Furth, H. G. (1970) *Piaget for Teachers*. Englewood Cliffs, New Jersey: Prentice Hall.

Gibson, Eleanor J. (1969) *Principles of Perceptual Learning and Development*. New York: Appleton Century Crofts.

Giglioli, Pier Paolo (ed.) (1972) *Language and Social Context*. Harmondsworth, Middlesex: Penguin.

Ginsberg, H. and Opper, S. (1969) *Piaget's Theory of Intellectual Development: An Introduction*. Englewood Cliffs, New Jersey: Prentice Hall.

Herriot, Peter (1970) *An Introduction to the Psychology of Language*. London: Methuen.

Lenneberg, E. H. (ed.) (1964) *New Directions in the Study of Language*. Cambridge, Mass: M.I.T. Press.

Lloyd, Barbara B. (1972) *Perception and Cognition*. Harmondsworth, Middlesex: Penguin.

McNeill, D. (1970) *The Acquisition of Language: The Study of Developmental Psycholinguistics*. New York: Harper and Row.

Menyuk, P. (1971) *The Acquisition and Development of Language*. Englewood Cliffs, New Jersey: Prentice Hall.

Moore, Timothy E. (ed.) (1973) *Cognitive Development and the Acquisition of Language*. New York: Academic Press.

Oldfield, R. C. and Marshall, J. C. (eds.) (1968) *Language*. Harmondsworth, Middlesex: Penguin.

Smith, Frank and Miller, George A. (eds.) (1966) *The Genesis of Language*. Cambridge, Mass.: M.I.T. Press.

Society for Research in Child Development. (1970) *Cognitive Development in Children*. (Five monographs) Chicago: University of Chicago Press.

Vygotsky, Lev Semenovich (1962) *Thought and Language*. Cambridge, Mass.: M.I.T. Press.

References
and Name Index

The numbers in italics following each entry refer to page numbers within this book.

Adams, R. (1972) *Watership Down*. London: Puffin. *86*

Berko-Gleason, Jean, (1973) Code switching in Children's language. In Timothy E. Moore (ed.) *Cognitive Development and the Acquisition of Language*. New York: Academic Press, 159–67. *122, 123*

Berlyne, D. E. (1954) A theory of human curiosity. *British Journal of Psychology* 45:180–91. *35*

Berlyne, D. E. (1962a) Comments on relations between Piaget's theory and S-R theory. *Society for Research in Child Development Monograph* 27(2):127–31. *36*

Berlyne, D. E. (1962b) Uncertainty and epistemic curiosity. *British Journal of Psychology* 53:27–34. *35*

Berlyne, D. E. (1963) Soviet research on intellectual processes in children. *Society for Research in Child Development Monograph* 28(2):165–83. *36, 37*

Berlyne, D. E. (1965) *Structure and Direction in Thinking*. New York: John Wiley. *33, 34*

Bernstein, B. (1971) *Theoretical Studies towards a Sociology of Language*. Vol. 1 of *Class, Codes and Control*. London: Routledge and Kegan Paul. *125–8, 130*

Bloom, L. M. (1970) *Language, Development: Form and Function in Emerging Grammars*. Cambridge, Mass.: M.I.T. Press. *101, 112*

Bloom, L. M. (1973) Why not pivot grammar? In C. A. Ferguson and Dan. I. Slobin (eds.) *Studies of Child Language and Development*. New York: Holt, Rinehart and Winston. *108*

Blount, B. G. (1969) Acquisition of language by Luo children. *Working Paper No. 19, Language Behaviour Research Laboratory*. Berkeley: University of California. *96*

Boring, Edwin G. (ed.) (1952) *A History of Psychology in Autobiography Vol. 4*. New York: Russell and Russell. *22*

Bower, T. G. R. (1966) Heterogeneous summation in human infants. *Animal Behaviour 14*:395–8. *67*

Bower, T. G. R. (1974) *Development in Infancy*. San Francisco: W. H. Freeman. *52, 65, 66, 67, 71, 75, 76, 77*

Bower, T. G. R., Broughton, J. M., and Moore, M. K. (1971) Infant responses to approaching object: an indicator of response to distal variables. *Perception and Psychophysics 9*:193–6. *66*

Bower, T. G. R., and Wishart, J. G. (1973) *Development of Auditory Manual Co-ordination*. (In preparation) *65*

Bowerman, Melissa (1973) Structural relationships in children's utterances, syntactic or semantic. In Timothy E. Moore (ed.) *Cognitive Development and the Acquisition of Language*. New York: Academic Press. *107, 112, 113*

Braine, Martin D. S. (1963) The ontogeny of English phrase structure: the first phase. *Language 39*:1–14. *96*

Brandis, W. S., and Henderson, D. (1970) *Social Class, Language and Communication*. London: Routledge and Kegan Paul.

Brown, Roger (1973) *A First Language*. London: George Allen and Unwin. *87, 93, 94, 101, 107, 111, 113, 114, 120*

Brown, Roger, and Bellugi, Ursula (1964) Three processes in the child's acquisition of syntax. *Harvard Educational Review 34*(2):133–51. *97, 118*

Brown, Roger, and Hanlon, Camille (1970) Derivational complexity and order of acquisition in child speech. In John R. Hayes (ed.) *Cognition and the Development of Language*. New York: John Wiley. *120*

Bruner, Jerome S. (1957a) On perceptual readiness. *Psychological Review 64*:123–52 (Reproduced in Bruner, 1973). *49*

Bruner, Jerome S. (1957b) Going beyond the information given. In Bruner *et al. Contemporary Approaches to Cognition*. Cambridge, Mass.: Harvard University Press (Reproduced in Bruner, 1973).

Bruner, Jerome S. (1964) The course of cognitive growth. *American Psychologist 19*:1–15. (Reproduced in Bruner, 1973).

Bruner, Jerome S. (1971) The growth and structure of skill. In

K. J. Connolly (ed.) *Motor Skills in Infancy*. London: Academic Press (Reproduced in Bruner, 1973). *41*

Bruner, Jerome S. (1973) *Beyond the Information Given*. London: George Allen and Unwin. *40, 42, 46*

Bruner, Jerome S., and Goodman, Cecile C. (1947) Value and need as organizing factors in perception. *Journal of Abnormal and Social Psychology 42*(1):33–34.

Bruner, Jerome S., Goodnow, Jacqueline S., and Austin, George A. (1956) *A Study of Thinking*. New York: John Wiley (Science Edn. 1962). *71, 72, 73*

Bruner, Jerome S., and Kenney, H. (1966) The development of the concepts of order and proportion in children. In Bruner *et al* (eds.) *Studies in Cognitive Growth*. New York: John Wiley. *43, 71*

Bruner, Jerome S., Olver, Rose R., and Greenfield, Patricia, M. *et al*. (1966) *Studies in Cognitive Growth*. New York: John Wiley. *40*

Bryant, Peter (1974) *Perception and Understanding in Young Children*. London: Methuen.

Campbell, Robin, and Wales, Roger (1970) The study of language acquisition. In John Lyons (ed.) *New Horizons in Linguistics*. Harmondsworth, Middlesex: Penguin. *117, 118, 119*

Cazden, C. (1965) *Environmental Assistance to the Child's Acquisition of Grammar*. Unpublished doctoral dissertation, Harvard University. *119*

Cazden, C. (1968) The acquisition of noun and verb inflections. *Child Development 39*:433–48. *119*

Chomsky, C. (1969) *The Acquisition of Syntax in Children from Five to Ten*. Cambridge, Mass.: M.I.T. Press. *110, 111*

Chomsky, N. (1959) A review of B. F. Skinner's *Verbal Behaviour*. *Language 55*:26–58. *95*

Chomsky, N. (1965) *Aspects of the Theory of Syntax*. Cambridge, Mass.: M.I.T. Press. *92, 97*

Clark, Eve V. (1973a) What's in a word? On the child's acquisition of semantics in his first language. In Timothy E. Moore (ed.) *Cognitive Development and the Acquisition of Language*. New York: Academic Press. *113*

Clark, Eve V. (1973b) How children describe time and order. In Charles A. Ferguson and Dan I. Slobin (eds.) *Studies of Child Language and Development*. New York: Holt, Rinehart, and Winston. *123, 124, 126*

Clark, Herbert H. (1973) Space, time, semantics and the child. In Timothy E. Moore (ed.) *Cognitive Development and the Acquisition of Language*. New York: Academic Press. *88*

Cromer, Richard F. (1974) The development of language and cognition: the cognition hypothesis. In Brian Foss (ed.) *New Perspectives in Child Development*. Harmondsworth, Middlesex: Penguin. *108*

Dodd, B. (1972) Effects of social and vocal stimulation on infant babbling. *Developmental Psychology* 7:80–3. *120*

Donaldson, M., and Balfour, G. (1968) Less is more: a study of language comprehension in children. *British Journal of Psychology* 59:461–71. *89*

Dracht, K., Kobashigawa, B., Pfuderer, C., and Slobin, D. (1969) The structure of linguistic input to children. *Language Behaviour Research Laboratory, Working Paper 14*. Berkeley: University of California. *118*

Ervin, Susan M. (1964) Imitation and structural change in children's language. In Eric H. Lenneberg (ed.) *New Directions in the Study of Language*. Cambridge, Mass.: M.I.T. Press. *121*

Ervin-Tripp, S. M. (1966) Language development. In L. W. and M. L. Hoffman (eds.) *Review of Child Development*. New York: Russell Sage Foundation. *114*

Ervin-Tripp, S. M. (1973) Some strategies for the first two years. In Timothy E. Moore (ed.) *Cognitive Development and the Acquisition of Language*. New York: Academic Press. *96*

Fantz, Robert L. (1961) The origin of form perception. *Scientific American*, 204(5):66–72. *62, 63*

Fantz, Robert L. (1966) Pattern discrimination and selective attention as determinants of perceptual development from birth. In Aline H. Kidd and Jeanne L. Rivoire (eds.) *Perceptual Development in Children*. New York: International Universities Press. *62, 65*

Feldman, Carol F., and Rodgon, Maris (1970) *The Effects of Various Types of Adult Responses in the Syntactic Acquisitions of Two to Three Year Olds*. Unpublished Paper, Department of Psychology, University of Chicago. *119*

Ferguson, Charles A., and Slobin, Dan I. (eds.) (1973) *Studies of Child Language Development*. New York: Holt, Rinehart and Winston. *106, 114*

Fraser, C., Bellugi, U., and Brown, Roger (1963) Control of grammar in imitation, comprehension and production. *Journal of Verbal Learning and Verbal Behaviour* 2:121–35. *120, 125*

Garnica, Olga G. (1973) The development of phonemic speech perception. In Timothy E. Moore (ed.) *Cognitive Development and the Acquisition of Language*. New York: Academic Press. *104*

Gesell, A., Thompson, H., and Amatruda, C. S. (1934) *Infant Behaviour: its Genesis and Growth.* New York: McGraw Hill. *65*

Gibson, Eleanor J. (1963) Development of perception: discrimination of depth compared with discrimination of graphic symbols. *Society for Research in Child Development Monograph 28*(2): 5–24. *60, 61, 62, 64*

Gibson, J. J. (1950) *The Perception of the Visual World.* Cambridge: Riverside Press. *52*

Goodnow, J. J. (1969) Problems in research on culture and thought. In D. Elkind and J. H. Flavell (eds.) *Studies in Cognitive Development.* Oxford University Press. *80*

Gréco, P. (1962) Quantité et quotité. In P. Gréco and A. Morf, *Etudes d'Epistemologie Génétique 13*: 1–70. Paris: Presses Universitaires de France. *78*

Green, Donald Ross, Ford, Marquerite P., and Flames, George B. (eds.) (1971) *Measurement and Piaget.* New York: McGraw Hill. *25*

Greenfield, Patricia M. (1966) On culture and conversation. In J. S. Bruner, Rose R. Olver, Patricia M. Greenfield, *et al* (eds.) *Studies in Cognitive Growth.* New York: John Wiley. *46*

Gvozdev, A. N. (1961) *Problems in the Language Development of the Child.* Moscow: Academy of Pediatric Science. *112*

Halliday, M. A. K. (1975) *Learning How to Mean.* London: Edward Arnold. *101, 102, 115, 116, 117*

Hess, Robert D., and Shipman, Virginia C. (1965) Early experience and the socialization of cognitive modes in children. *Child Development 34*(4): 869–86. *129*

Hull, Clarke Leonard (1943) *Principles of Behaviour: An Introduction to Behaviour Theory.* New York: Appleton. *35*

Hyde, D. M. G. (1970) *Piaget and Conceptual Development.* London: Holt, Rinehart, and Winston. *79*

Inhelder, B. (1962) Some aspects of Piaget's genetic approach to cognition. In *Society for Research in Child Development, Monograph 27*(2): 19–34. *15, 23*

James, W. (1890) *The Principles of Psychology.* New York: Holt. *42*

Kaplan, Eleanor L. (1969) *The Role of Intonation in the Acquisition of Language.* Unpublished doctoral dissertation, Cornell University.

Kendler, H., and Kendler, Tracy S. (1962) Vertical and horizontal processes in problem-solving. *Psychological Review 69*: 1–16. *31, 32, 36*

Kernan, K. T. (1969) *The Acquisition of Language by Samoan*

Children. Unpublished doctoral dissertation, University of California, Berkeley.

Klein, S. P. (1963) *A Developmental Study of Tactual Perception*. Unpublished doctoral dissertation, Clerk University. *57*

Klima, Edwards, and Bellugi, Ursula (1966) Syntactic regularities in the speech of children. In J. Lyons and R. J. Wales (eds.) *Psycholinguistics Papers*. Edinburgh University Press. *108*

Kuhlman, Clementina (1960) *Visual Imagery in Children*. Unpublished doctoral dissertation, Harvard University.

Lenneberg, E. H. (1964) A biological perspective of language. In E. H. Lenneberg (ed.) *New Directions in the Study of Language*. Cambridge, Mass.: M.I.T. Press. *98, 99, 100*

Lenneberg, E. H. (1967) *Biological Foundations of Language*. New York: John Wiley. *98, 99, 100*

Limber, John (1973) The genesis of complex sentences. In Timothy E. Moore (ed.) *Cognitive Development and the Acquisition of Language*. New York: Academic Press. *111*

Lind, J. H., Truby, H. M., and Bosma, J. F. (1965) *Newborn Infant Cry*. Upsala: Alquist and Wiesells. *90*

Luria, A. R. (1961) *The Role of Speech in the Regulation of Normal and Abnormal Behaviour*. Oxford: Pergamon Press.

McGurk, H. (1974) Visual perception in young infants. In Brian Foss (ed.) *New Perspectives in Child Development*. Hammondsworth, Middlesex: Penguin. *67*

McKenzie, B. E. and Day, R. H. (1972) Object distance as a determinant of visual fixation in early infancy. *Science 178*: 1108–10. *65*

McNeill, David (1966) Developmental psycholinguistics. In Frank Smith and George A. Millar (eds.) *The Genesis of Language*. Cambridge, Mass.: M.I.T. Press. *95, 98, 120*

McNeill, David (1970a) *The Acquisition of Language: The Study of Developmental Psycholinguistics*. New York: Harper and Row.

McNeill, David (1970b) The development of language. In Paul Mussen (ed.) *Carmichael's Manual of Child Psychology, Vol. 1*. New York: John Wiley. *97, 107*

Menyuk, Paula (1971) *The Acquisition and Development of Language*. Englewood Cliffs, New Jersey: Prentice Hall.

Menyuk, P., and Bernholtz, N. (1969) Prosodic features and child's language production. *Research Laboratory of Electronics, Quarterly Progress Report, No.* 93. *106*

Miller, N. E. (1948) Studies of fear as an acquirable drive: 1. Fear as motivation and fear-reduction as reinforcement in the learning of new responses. *Journal of Experimental Psychology* 38:89–101. *31*

Moore, Timothy E. (ed.) (1973) *Cognitive Development and the Acquisition of Language.* New York: Academic Press.

Olson, David R. (1966) On conceptual strategies. In J. S. Bruner, Rose R. Olver, Patricia M. Greenfield *et al. Studies in Cognitive Growth.* New York: John Wiley. *73*

Papousek, H. (1969) Individual variability in learned responses in human infants. In R. J. Robinson (ed) *Brian and Early Behaviour.* New York: Academic Press.

Pavlovitch, M. (1920) *Le Language enfantin: acquisition du serbe et du français par un enfant serbe.* Paris: Champion. *113, 114*

Piaget, J. (1930) *The Child's Conception of Physical Causality.* London, Routledge and Kegan Paul. *82, 83, 84*

Piaget, J. (1946a) *Le développement de la notion de temps chez l'enfant.* Paris: Presses Universitaires de France. *81, 82*

Piaget, J. (1946b) *Les Notions de mouvement et de vitesse chez L'enfant.* Paris: Presses Universitaires de France. *82*

Piaget, J. (1949) *La Formation du symbole.* Neuchâtel: Delachaux et Nièstle. *88*

Piaget, J. (1951) *Play, Dreams, and Imitations in Childhood.* New York: W. W. Norton. *75*

Piaget, J. (1952) *The Child's Conception of Number.* New York: Humanities Press. *78*

Piaget, J. (1953) *The Origin of Intelligence in the Child.* London: Routledge and Kegan Paul. *14, 17, 75*

Piaget, J. (1955) *The Construction of Reality in the Child.* London: Routledge and Kegan Paul. *75*

Piaget, J. (1958) *The Growth of Logical Thinking.* London: Routledge and Kegan Paul. *24*

Piaget, J. (1969) *The Mechanisms of Perception.* New York: Basic Books. *48*

Piaget, J., and Inhelder, B. (1963) *The Child's Conception of Space.* London: Routledge and Kegan Paul.

Potter, Mary C. (1966) On perceptual recognition. In J. S. Bruner, Rose Olver, Patricia Greenfield *et al. Studies in Cognitive Growth.* New York: John Wiley. *58*

Preston, M., and Yeni-Komshian (1967) *Studies of Development of Stop Consonants in Children.* Hoskins Laboratories SR-11. *104*

Price-Williams, D. R., Gordon, W., and Ramirez, W. (1969) Skill and conservation: a study of pottery-makers' children. *Developmental Psychology 1*:769. *80*

Rheingold, Harriet L., Gerwitz, Jacob L., and Ross, Helen W. (1959) Social conditioning of vocalizations in the infant. *Journal of Comparative and Physiological Psychology 52*:68–78. *90*

Ricks, D. M. (1972) *The Beginnings of Vocal Communication in*

Infants and Autistic Children. Unpublished doctorate of medicine thesis, University of London. *120*

Schlesinger, I. M. (1971) Production of utterances and language acquisition. In Dan I. Slobin (ed.) *The Ontogenesis of Grammar*. New York: Academic Press. *112*

Schvachkin, N. (1948) Development of phonemic speech perception in early childhood. In Elena Derntach, C. H. Ferguson, and Dan I. Slobin (eds.) *Studies of Child Language Development*. New York: Holt, Rinehart and Winston. *104*

Sinclair-de-Zwart, H. (1973) Language acquisition and cognitive development. In Timothy E. Moore (ed.), *Cognitive Development and the Acquisition of Language*. New York: Academic Press. *88*

Slobin, Dan I. (1964) *Imitation and the Acquisition of Syntax*. Paper presented at second planning conference of Project Literacy. *119*

Slobin, Dan I. (1971) Developmental psycholinguistics. In William Orr Dingwall (ed.) *A Survey of Linguistic Science*. College Park Maryland, William Orr Dingwall Linguistics Program: University of Maryland.

Slobin, Dan I. (1972) Seven questions about language development. In P. C. Dodwell (ed.) *New Horizons in Psychology 2*. Harmondsworth, Middlesex: Penguin. *111*

Slobin, Dan I. (1973) Cognitive pre-requisites for the development of grammar. In Charles A. Ferguson and Dan I. Slobin (eds.) *Studies of Child Language Development*. New York: Holt, Rinehart and Winston. *89*

Smith, Carlota S. (1970) An experimental approach to children's linguistic competence. In John R. Hayes (ed.) *Cognition and the Development of Language*. New York: John Wiley. *109*

Sonstroem, Anne Mackinnon (1966) On the conservation of solids. In J. S. Bruner, Rose R. Olver, Patricia Greenfield *et al. Studies in Cognitive Growth*. New York: John Wiley. *45*

Tonkova-Yampol'skaya (1968) Development of speech intonation in infants during the first two years of life. In Charles A. Ferguson and Dan I. Slobin (eds.) *Studies of Child Language Development*. New York: Holt, Rinehart and Winston (1973). *105*

Vygotsky, Lev Semenovich (1962) *Thought and Language*. Cambridge, Mass.: M.I.T. Press. *69, 70, 71, 88, 90*

Watson, John S. (1968) Conservation: an S.R. analysis. In Irvin E. Sigel and Frank H. Hooper (eds.) *Logical Thinking in Children*. London: Holt, Rinehart and Winston. *29, 30*

Werner, H. (1957) The concept of development from a comparative organismic point of view. In D. Harris (ed.) *The Concept of Development: An Issue in the Study of Human Behaviour.* Minneapolis: University of Minnesota.   *37*

Werner, H., and Kaplan, E. (1952) Acquisition of word meanings: a developmental study. *Society for Research in Child Development, Monograph 15*:190–200.   *38*

Werner, H., and Kaplan, E. (1963). *Symbol Formation: An Organismic-Developmental Approach to Language and the Expression of Thought,* New York: John Wiley.   *38*

Wertheimer, M. (1962) Psychomotor co-ordination of auditory-visual space at birth. *Science 134.*   *65*

Wohlwill, Joachim F. (1962) From perception to inference: a dimension of cognitive development. *Society for Research in Child Development Monograph 27*(2):87–107.   *50, 51*

Zaporozhets, A. V. (1965) The development of perception in the pre-school child. *Society for Research in Child Development Monograph 30*(2):82–101.

Zhurova, L. Ye (1963) The development of analysis of words into their sounds by pre-school children. In Charles A. Ferguson and Dan I. Slobin (eds.) *Studies of Child Language Development.* New York: Holt, Rinehart and Winston (1973).   *104*

Subject Index

accommodation, 14, 16, 26
adaptation, 14, 15, 16, 26
assimilation, 14, 16, 26
auto-kinetic effect, 52, 53
babbling, 90, 91, 104, 120
cardination, 77, 78
circular reaction, 17
  primary, 17
  secondary, 17
classification, 20, 22, 23, 42, 68,
  77, 78, 82
code/codes/coding, 43, 122, 125,
  126, 127, 130
cognition structures, 13, 14, 15,
  16, 25, 26
competence
  communicative, 87, 118, 125
  linguistic, 86, 87, 92, 98, 110,
  125, 130, 131
comprehension, 109, 110, 120,
  121, 122
concept, 16, 67, 68, 69, 70, 71,
  75, 85
  of causality, 69, 81, 82, 84, 85
  of number, 68, 77, 78, 79, 80, 82
  semantic, 113
  of space, 68
  of time, 68, 69, 81, 82
concept attainment, 71
  concrete operations, 16, 21, 22,
  23

concrete, stage, 23
conflict, 34
conservation, 19, 20, 29, 45, 46,
  80, 81, 85
deep structure, 92, 98, 100, 112,
  124
distance perception, 65, 66
egocentric, 19, 21
enactive representation, 43, 45
environment, 11, 12, 13, 14, 15,
  16, 17, 26, 38, 43, 47, 64, 68,
  69, 80, 97, 99, 100, 104
  linguistic, 116
equilibration, 15, 26, 35
equilibrium, 14, 15, 16
expansion, 118, 119, 122, 123,
  125
form perception, 62
formal operations, 16, 21, 23, 24,
  26
formal thought, 24, 26
function, linguistic, 101, 115, 116,
  131
grammar, 90, 96
  case, 92, 93
  transformational, 92, 93
grammatical relations, 88, 112
iconic representation, 43, 44, 45
imitation, 95, 119, 120, 121, 122,
  123, 124, 125
innate, 97, 98, 107